KB037666

Essential VOCA with Stories

2

Essential VOCA with Stories 2

Written by Michael A. Putlack • Elizabeth Lee

First Published August 2020

Publisher: Kyudo Chung
Editors: Ziin Zong
Designers: Miju Yoon, Miyoung Lim
Photo Credit: www.shutterstock.com

Published and distributed by Happy House, an imprint of DARAKWON
Darakwon Bldg., 211 Moonbal-ro, Paju-si Gyeonggi-do, Korea 10881
Tel: 82-2-736-2031(Ext. 250) **Fax:** 82-2-732-2037 **Homepage:** www.ihappyhouse.co.kr

Copyright© 2020, Michael A. Putlack
All rights reserved.
No part of this publication may be reproduced, stored in a retrieval system, or transmitted in any form or by any means, electronic, mechanical, photocopying or otherwise, without the prior consent of the copyright owner. Refund after purchase is possible only according to the company regulations. Contact the above telephone number for any inquiries. Consumer damages caused by loss, damage, etc. can be compensated according to the consumer dispute resolution standards announced by the Korea Fair Trade Commission. An incorrectly collated book will be exchanged.

ISBN: 978-89-6653-574-3 63740
Age Range: 12 years and up
Price: ₩14,000

Components
Student Book

Free Downloadable Resources at www.ihappyhouse.co.kr
Answer Key & Translation • MP3 Files • Audio Script • Word List • Word Test

Essential VOCA

with Stories

2

Happy House

Table of Contents

How to Use This Book 6

Unit 01	atmosphere, blossom, caterpillar, climate, countryside, creature, greenhouse, harvest, horizon, insect, landmark, liquid, outdoor, pleasant, pollute, scenery, settle, sight, typhoon, underground	8
Unit 02	amaze, anger, anxious, ashamed, bother, cheerful, curious, dull, foolish, gentle, grateful, happiness, personality, reasonable, regret, shock, uneasy, unhappy, useless, wisdom	12
Unit 03	active, appointment, cancer, cause, chemical, deaf, death, digest, drug, experiment, function, growth, harm, hunger, lively, medical, nutrition, physical, recover, relax	16
Unit 04	advertise, allowance, benefit, bet, billion, budget, business, capital, charge, expense, gain, income, opportunity, period, poverty, quarter, resource, salary, shopkeeper, support	20
Unit 05	abroad, available, border, castle, coast, comfort, cost, cultural, encounter, fortunate, journey, local, native, nearby, observe, passenger, preserve, remain, sightseeing, village	24
Review 01		28

Unit 06	admire, apologize, argue, awkward, behave, blame, community, conversation, disagree, frankly, generous, ignore, inspire, lifetime, marry, passion, professional, relationship, responsible, worried	32
Unit 07	achieve, average, cheat, clever, compete, concentrate, excellent, genius, information, progress, pronounce, purpose, research, review, solution, subtract, system, teenager, textbook, total	36
Unit 08	architect, astronaut, athlete, author, compose, conductor, dedication, diligent, engineer, equipment, focus, influence, intelligent, invent, manage, newspaper, organize, performance, role, successful	40
Unit 09	animation, attractive, audience, background, cancel, celebration, choir, decorate, exhibit, hobby, mystery, novel, pretend, probably, publish, realistic, script, situation, technology, vivid	44
Unit 10	aim, arrow, attack, campaign, capture, command, damage, destroy, empire, guard, independence, invade, kill, mission, obstacle, risk, shoot, soldier, victory, violent	48
Review 02		52

Unit 11	artificial, century, clearly, electric, extreme, forecast, imagine, increase, incredible, laboratory, microwave, modern, operation, satellite, scientific, spaceship, telescope, transport, vehicle, vision	56
Unit 12	accident, amount, arrest, bad, bite, bullet, careless, disabled, earthquake, emergency, hit, mess, panic, paralyze, prison, scare, scream, tragedy, unbelievable, worse	60
Unit 13	able, alive, cough, fat, freeze, injury, miracle, overweight, pimple, poison, proper, provide, rapidly, relieve, sneeze, soap, sunlight, tissue, wound, youth	64
Unit 14	actual, appear, brief, deeply, differ, ease, elder, equal, hug, nickname, normal, opposite, pair, patient, personal, private, realize, respect, similar, terrific	68
Unit 15	avenue, construction, describe, downstairs, drawer, exit, front, furniture, handkerchief, heritage, item, niece, property, repair, spare, supper, swing, usual, warm, within	72
Review 03		76

Unit 16	absorb, aloud, aware, beauty, bitter, calm, clap, dirty, feather, flow, fur, heat, nod, pour, quality, raw, rub, smooth, squeeze, unusual	80
Unit 17	adapt, affect, ancient, common, conclusion, debate, detail, discover, discuss, documentary, education, expert, figure, lecture, principal, riddle, scholar, suppose, survey, valuable	84
Unit 18	apply, appoint, article, cash, congratulate, customer, department, disadvantage, goods, interview, law, practical, presentation, regular, reply, separate, serve, supply, tax, wealthy	88
Unit 19	allow, chase, compare, custom, encourage, exist, fact, generally, host, include, instruct, list, nearly, notice, particular, safety, since, typical, unlike, weekly	92
Unit 20	adopt, attempt, chief, chore, determine, develop, disappear, impress, inform, memorize, method, owner, precious, produce, recognize, reflect, spot, survive, tool, value	96
Review 04		100

Unit 21	appreciate, backward, concern, connect, consider, demand, disappoint, emotion, hesitate, insult, measure, option, persuade, promise, relative, scene, selfish, shy, sincere, whisper	104
Unit 22	area, base, beg, bottom, continent, crowd, distance, divide, familiar, fence, ideal, illegal, official, population, president, slave, species, tribe, unit, worth	108
Unit 23	bare, beard, cell, chest, elbow, exactly, footprint, huge, imitate, infect, lower, lung, organic, position, power, race, stomach, thumb, whole	112
Unit 24	attract, cart, continue, display, electronic, flavor, found, gift, jewel, mail, metal, object, order, owe, pack, refuse, return, sample, steal, various	116
Unit 25	behind, bubble, certain, code, dare, enemy, escape, fortunately, guess, handle, joy, length, magic, monster, original, perform, release, source, treasure, war	120
Review 05		124

Unit 26	blend, cave, dew, dive, entrance, flight, grain, ground, harbor, north, planet, polar, rare, root, seafood, shell, shore, southern, tomb, universe	128
Unit 27	depend, die, emerge, except, fear, force, god, hide, justice, liberty, movement, path, plenty, poor, proverb, rent, sense, stage, sudden, tide	132
Unit 28	bump, concrete, crack, dirt, evidence, false, form, humorous, indoor, joke, lunar, male, medium, positive, royal, sticky, terribly, western, wood	136
Unit 29	bow, direct, disturb, expect, grab, hardly, knock, lock, neat, nowadays, obey, portrait, prefer, senior, shelter, shout, suggest, tend, vet, wrap	140
Unit 30	bill, cast, consonant, elect, envelope, fare, idiom, march, motto, offer, prevent, prove, rate, scale, score, section, site, skip, staff, vowel	144
Review 06		148

Index 153

How to Use This Book

Target Words

This section contains 20 target words. Comprehensive information about each word is provided. This includes the part of speech, one or more definitions, and one or more expressions that contain the word. There is also one or more sample sentence using the word, so readers can see how to use the word properly.

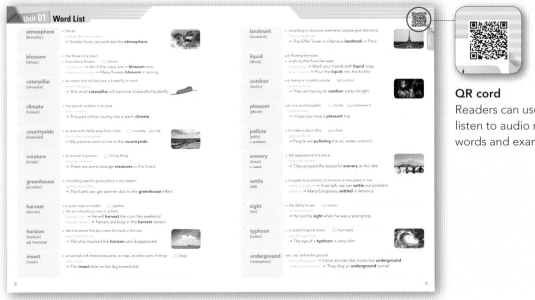

QR cord

Readers can use the QR code to listen to audio recordings of the words and examples sentences.

Unit Exercises

There are a wide variety of exercises for readers to practice the words they learn in Word List. The exercises give readers the opportunity to test their knowledge of the definitions of the words and how the words are used in sentences. There is also a short reading passage containing target words from the unit. Following it are 4 comprehension questions to make sure that readers understand the passage.

Review Units

After every five units, there is a review unit. This section retests readers on the knowledge they learned in the previous units. There are exercises that test readers on definitions and word usage. Each review unit also contains a crossword puzzle and a reading passage containing target words. Readers must then answer comprehension questions testing their understanding of the passage.

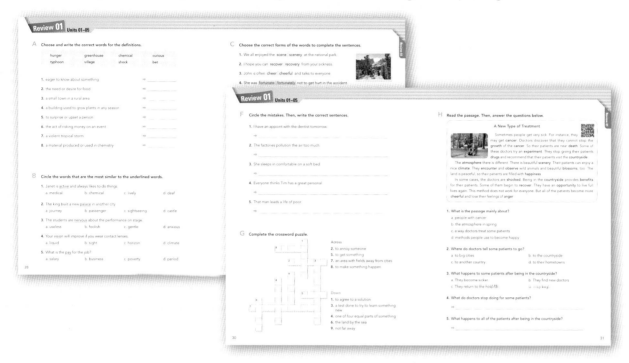

Index

The index contains all of the words in each unit. Readers can use it to search for words while studying.

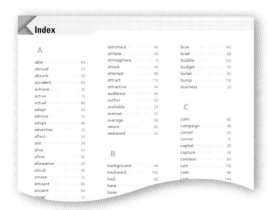

Answer Key & Translation

The answer key and Korean translation may be downloaded for free at www.ihappyhouse.co.kr.

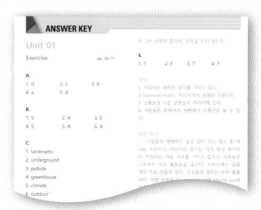

Part of Speech Abbreviations	• noun = *n.* • verb = *v.* • adjective = *adj.* • adverb = *adv.*
	• preposition = *prep.* • pronoun = *pron.* • conjunction = *con.*

1 atmosphere
[ǽtməsfìər]

n. the air
pollute the atmosphere
→ Smoke from cars pollutes the **atmosphere**.

2 blossom
[blásəm]

n. the flower of a plant
v. to produce flowers   (syn) bloom
in blossom → All of the roses are in **blossom** now.
blossom in spring → Many flowers **blossom** in spring.

3 caterpillar
[kǽtərpìlər]

n. an insect that will become a butterfly or moth
small caterpillar
→ The small **caterpillar** will become a beautiful butterfly.

4 climate
[kláimət]

n. the typical weather in an area
warm climate
→ This part of the country has a warm **climate**.

5 countryside
[kʌ́ntrisàid]

n. an area with fields away from cities   (syn) country   (ant) city
live in the countryside
→ My parents want to live in the **countryside**.

6 creature
[krí:tʃər]

n. an animal or person   (syn) living thing
strange creature
→ There are some strange **creatures** in the forest.

7 greenhouse
[grí:nhàus]

n. a building used to grow plants in any season
greenhouse effect
→ The Earth can get warmer due to the **greenhouse** effect.

8 harvest
[há:rvist]

v. to pick crops in a field   (syn) gather
n. the act of picking crops in a field
harvest corn → He will **harvest** the corn this weekend.
harvest season → Famers are busy in the **harvest** season.

9 horizon
[həráizən]
adj. horizontal

n. the line where the sky meets the land or the sea
reach the horizon
→ The ship reached the **horizon** and disappeared.

10 insect
[ínsekt]

n. an animal with three body parts, six legs, and two pairs of wings   (syn) bug
insect bite
→ The **insect** bite on her leg turned red.

11 **landmark**
[lǽndmà:rk]

n. a building or structure used when people give directions

famous landmark

→ The Eiffel Tower is a famous **landmark** in Paris.

---

12 **liquid**
[líkwid]

adj. flowing like water

n. anything that flows like water

liquid soap → Wash your hands with **liquid** soap.

pour a liquid → Pour the **liquid** into the bottle.

---

13 **outdoor**
[áutdò:r]

adj. being or located outside   ant indoor

outdoor party

→ They are having an **outdoo**r party tonight.

---

14 **pleasant**
[plézənt]

adj. nice and enjoyable   syn lovely   ant unpleasant

pleasant trip

→ I hope you have a **pleasant** trip.

---

15 **pollute**
[pəlú:t]

n. pollution

v. to make a place dirty   ant clean

pollute the air

→ People are **polluting** the air, water, and soil.

---

16 **scenery**
[sí:nəri]

n. scene

n. the appearance of a place

beautiful scenery

→ They enjoyed the beautiful **scenery** at the lake.

---

17 **settle**
[sétl]

v. to agree to a solution; to move to a new place to live

settle a problem → If we talk, we can **settle** our problem.

settle in → Many Europeans **settled** in America.

---

18 **sight**
[sait]

n. the ability to see   syn vision

lose one's sight

→ He lost his **sight** when he was a young boy.

---

19 **typhoon**
[taifú:n]

n. a violent tropical storm   syn hurricane

eye of a typhoon

→ The eye of a **typhoon** is very calm.

---

20 **underground**
[ʌ̀ndərgráund]

adv. / adj. below the ground

live underground → Some animals like moles live **underground**.

underground tunnel → They dug an **underground** tunnel.

Unit 01

A Circle the words that fit the definitions.

1. a violent tropical storm

    a. horizon   b. climate   c. creature   d. typhoon

2. to produce flowers

    a. settle   b. harvest   c. blossom   d. pollute

3. the appearance of a place

    a. countryside   b. scenery   c. landmark   d. insect

4. an insect that will become a butterfly or moth

    a. caterpillar   b. greenhouse   c. atmosphere   d. sight

5. flowing like water

    a. underground   b. pleasant   c. outdoor   d. liquid

B Write S for synonym or A for antonym next to each pair of words.

1. _____ creature – living thing   **2.** _____ outdoor – indoor

3. _____ insect – bug   **4.** _____ harvest – gather

5. _____ countryside – city   **6.** _____ pollute – clean

C Circle the words that best fit the sentences.

1. Rome has many famous creatures | landmarks throughout the city.

2. The tunnel goes very deep underground | pleasant .

3. Please do not blossom | pollute the ground or water.

4. We grow tomatoes in winter in our greenhouse | harvest .

5. The climate | insect in this area is hot and rainy.

6. His family has a(n) liquid | outdoor swimming pool at their house.

D **Choose the correct words to complete the sentences.**

1. You can easily see the _____ at the beach.

   a. horizon   b. harvest   c. liquid   d. climate

2. They hope to _____ in England and live there.

   a. blossom   b. pollute   c. harvest   d. settle

3. She is kind and has a _____ personality.

   a. liquid   b. outdoor   c. pleasant   d. underground

4. The _____ is very dirty in some places.

   a. blossom   b. atmosphere   c. caterpillar   d. typhoon

5. Because his _____ is good, he does not wear glasses.

   a. countryside   b. creature   c. sight   d. scenery

E **Read the passage. Then, write T for true or F for false.**

 One popular place people like to travel to is Hawaii. The **atmosphere** in Hawaii is almost always **pleasant**. It has a hot **climate**, so people enjoy **outdoor** activities there. There are seven main islands in Hawaii. The **scenery** in all of them is incredible. Some islands have famous natural **landmarks** such as Diamond Head and Mauna Loa. People can see **blossoms** on trees in Hawaii all year long. **Insects** are always flying from flower to flower. There are many other interesting **creatures** living there, too.

   People love visiting the beach and looking out at the **horizon**. It is incredible to see. Some people love Hawaii so much that they never go home. Instead, they decide to **settle** there and stay in Hawaii for the rest of their lives.

1. Hawaii has a pleasant atmosphere.   _____

2. Diamond Head is a famous typhoon in Hawaii.   _____

3. Insects and other creatures live in Hawaii.   _____

4. People can see the horizon from the beach in Hawaii.   _____

1	**amaze** [əméiz] *adj.* amazing	*v.* to surprise someone amaze an audience → The magician **amazed** the audience with his show.
2	**anger** [ǽŋgər]	*n.* the feeling of being upset or mad in anger → John yelled at them in **anger**.
3	**anxious** [ǽŋkʃəs]	*adj.* feeling worried or concerned (syn) nervous feel anxious → Jeff feels **anxious** about his math test.
4	**ashamed** [əʃéimd]	*adj.* feeling embarrassed because of one's actions (ant) proud ashamed of oneself → I am **ashamed** of myself for failing the test.
5	**bother** [báðər]	*v.* to annoy someone (syn) trouble bother someone → Please stop **bothering** me.
6	**cheerful** [tʃíərfəl] *v.* cheer	*adj.* happy or in a good mood (ant) sad cheerful smile → Her **cheerful** smile made everyone happy.
7	**curious** [kjú(:)əriəs] *n.* curiosity	*adj.* eager to know about something curious as a cat → Matt is as **curious** as a cat about everything.
8	**dull** [dʌl]	*adj.* not interesting; not bright (syn) boring (ant) exciting dull movie → I don't want to see this **dull** movie. dull colors → The painter used **dull** colors in the picture.
9	**foolish** [fúːliʃ]	*adj.* showing a lack of sense or wisdom (syn) silly (ant) wise foolish comment → Everyone laughed at her **foolish** comment.
10	**gentle** [dʒéntl]	*adj.* kind and calm (syn) nice (ant) violent gentle animal → A lamb is a **gentle** animal that does not bite.

11 grateful
[gréitfəl]

adj. very thankful for someone's kindness
grateful for
→ I am so **grateful** for all of your help.

12 happiness
[hǽpinis]

n. the state of being glad   ⟨syn⟩ pleasure   ⟨ant⟩ anger
full of happiness
→ Angela is always full of **happiness**.

13 personality
[pərsənǽləti]
adj. personal

n. the general way a person behaves   ⟨syn⟩ character
strong personality
→ My mother has a very strong **personality**.

14 reasonable
[ríːzənəbl]

adj. making sense
reasonable decision
→ My parents made a **reasonable** decision about our vacation.

15 regret
[rigrét]

v. to feel bad about a past action
regret a mistake
→ Sarah **regrets** the mistake she made last night.

16 shock
[ʃɑk]
adj. shocked

v. to surprise or upset a person
n. the feeling of being surprised
shock everyone → The loud noise **shocked** everyone.
major shock → His death was a major **shock** to the family.

17 uneasy
[ʌníːzi]

adj. feeling worried or unhappy about something   ⟨syn⟩ uncomfortable
feel uneasy
→ I feel **uneasy** about flying.

18 unhappy
[ʌnhǽpi]

adj. feeling sad or upset
unhappy life
→ Jack had an **unhappy** life as a child.

19 useless
[júːsləs]

adj. not having a purpose   ⟨syn⟩ worthless   ⟨ant⟩ useful
useless thing
→ Don't waste money buying **useless** things.

20 wisdom
[wízdəm]
adj. wise

n. knowledge of what is true and right
words of wisdom
→ My grandma gave me a few words of **wisdom**.

A **Match the words with their definitions.**

1. gentle •   • a. to surprise someone

2. useless •   • b. to feel bad about a past action

3. regret •   • c. kind and calm

4. anxious •   • d. the feeling of being surprised

5. amaze •   • e. feeling worried or concerned

6. anger •   • f. not interesting

7. shock •   • g. the feeling of being upset or mad

8. dull •   • h. not having a purpose

B **Circle the two words in each group that are opposites.**

1. a. curious   b. foolish   c. wise   d. unhappy

2. a. personality   b. wisdom   c. happiness   d. anger

3. a. proud   b. ashamed   c. gentle   d. useless

4. a. cheerful   b. reasonable   c. grateful   d. sad

C **Circle the words that best fit the sentences.**

1. She was grateful | anxious that someone helped her carry the boxes.

2. She said she was gentle | uneasy about the test.

3. Please do not bother | amaze me with constant phone calls.

4. The offer the salesperson made was reasonable | dull .

5. Tom was curious | ashamed when he forgot his lines in the play.

6. Mark was unhappy | foolish about losing his phone.

D **Choose the correct words to complete the sentences.**

1. Susan smiles a lot and is always very _____.

    a. ashamed   b. anxious   c. unhappy   d. cheerful

2. People can gain _____ through experience.

    a. anger   b. wisdom   c. shock   d. personality

3. I am _____ about how you got the tickets.

    a. curious   b. gentle   c. reasonable   d. dull

4. Some people have pleasant _____, so other people like them.

    a. personalities   b. shock   c. anger   d. happiness

5. She made a _____ mistake, so she got the problem wrong.

    a. grateful   b. useless   c. foolish   d. uneasy

E **Read the passage. Then, fill in the blanks.**

Jennifer was very **unhappy**. She had a test the next day. "Math is **useless**," she said to her father. "I don't want to **bother** studying it." Her father was **curious**. "Why do you think math is **useless**?" he asked. Jennifer thought for a minute. She was **shocked**. She could not think of an answer. "I feel a bit **foolish** now, Dad. I'll start studying."

The next day, Jennifer was **cheerful**. She was ready to take the test. She looked at her friends. Many of them looked **uneasy**. They were **anxious** about the test. But Jennifer was not. She answered all the questions correctly and got an A⁺ on the test. She was **amazed**. At home, she told her father, "Thanks for making me study, Dad. I feel really **grateful**."

1. Jennifer thought that math is _____.

2. Jennifer was _____ by her father's question.

3. Jennifer's friends felt anxious, so they looked _____.

4. Jennifer was _____ by her grade on the exam.

| 1 | **active**
[æktiv]
n. activity | *adj.* busy doing something physical   (syn) lively
active person
→ My brother is a very **active** person. |

| 2 | **appointment**
[əpɔ́intmənt]
v. appoint | *n.* a meeting set for a certain time and place
make an appointment
→ I made an **appointment** to see a dentist today. |

| 3 | **cancer**
[kǽnsər] | *n.* a disease that causes cells to grow in the body
lung cancer
→ He got lung **cancer** from smoking too much. |

| 4 | **cause**
[kɔːz] | *n.* the reason for a certain action   (syn) origin   (ant) result
v. to make something happen
major cause → Cars are a major **cause** of air pollution.
cause an accident → The heavy snow **caused** an accident. |

| 5 | **chemical**
[kémikəl] | *n.* a material produced or used in chemistry
adj. relating to chemistry
mix chemicals → Be careful when you mix **chemicals**.
chemical experiment → The scientist will do a **chemical** experiment. |

| 6 | **deaf**
[def] | *adj.* unable to hear anything
deaf person
→ A **deaf** person communicates with sign language. |

| 7 | **death**
[deθ]
adj. dead | *n.* the end of life   (ant) birth
sudden death
→ People were shocked by his sudden **death**. |

| 8 | **digest**
[daidʒést]
n. digestion | *v.* to turn food into nutrients in the body
digest food
→ This medicine helps people **digest** food easily. |

| 9 | **drug**
[drʌg] | *n.* something that treats a sick person   (syn) medicine
take a drug
→ Please take this **drug** three times a day. |

| 10 | **experiment**
[ikspérimənt] | *n.* a test done to try to learn something new
do an experiment
→ They will do an **experiment** in the lab. |

11 function
[fʌ́ŋkʃən]

n. a use of a piece of equipment   [syn] purpose
useful function
→ My smartphone has many useful **functions**.

12 growth
[grouθ]

n. the act of becoming bigger or larger   [syn] development
rapid growth
→ The city's rapid **growth** is amazing.

13 harm
[hɑːrm]

adj. harmful

v. to hurt or damage   [ant] heal
n. an injury or damage
harm someone → The dog **harmed** the woman by biting her.
cause harm → Pollution causes serious **harm** to people.

14 hunger
[hʌ́ŋɡər]

adj. hungry

n. the need or desire for food
experience hunger
→ I experienced **hunger** when I was lost in the desert.

15 lively
[láivli]

adj. full of life or energy   [syn] active
lively dance
→ They will do a **lively** dance at the festival.

16 medical
[médikəl]

adj. relating to medicine and the treatment of diseases
medical school
→ You must attend **medical** school to become a doctor.

17 nutrition
[njuːtríʃən]

n. the healthy material that someone gets from food
good nutrition
→ Good **nutrition** can help you grow quickly.

18 physical
[fízikəl]

adj. relating to the body   [ant] mental
physical activity
→ Regular **physical** activity is important.

19 recover
[rikʌ́vər]

n. recovery

v. to become well again after an illness   [syn] improve
recover one's health
→ Janet **recovered** her health thanks to the medicine.

20 relax
[riléks]

v. to rest
relax at the beach
→ Tom will **relax** at the beach during his vacation.

Unit 03 Exercise

A **Circle the words that fit the definitions.**

1. a material produced or used in chemistry

   a. function   b. chemical   c. drug   d. death

2. a test done to try to learn something new

   a. harm   b. cause   c. experiment   d. nutrition

3. unable to hear anything

   a. deaf   b. active   c. physical   d. medical

4. the need or desire for food

   a. death   b. hunger   c. function   d. appointment

5. a disease that causes cells to grow in the body

   a. growth   b. drug   c. nutrition   d. cancer

B **Choose and write the correct words for the blanks.**

lively	growth	cause	physical	death	harm

1. development = _____

2. mental ≠ _____

3. heal ≠ _____

4. active = _____

5. origin = _____

6. birth ≠ _____

C **Circle the words that best fit the sentences.**

1. His stomach hurts because he cannot digest | recover food well.

2. Eating food with lots of nutrition | hunger is good for the body.

3. Do you know how many experiments | functions this phone has?

4. Sharon sometimes causes | relaxes problems in her classroom.

5. They made an experiment | appointment to meet after lunch.

6. Try to relax | harm and not think about anything.

D **Choose the correct words to complete the sentences.**

1. The doctor gave the sick patient some _____ to take.
   a. functions   b. growth   c. drugs   d. appointment

2. It should take you five days to _____ from the illness.
   a. cause   b. recover   c. harm   d. digest

3. He is very _____ and loves to play sports.
   a. active   b. deaf   c. chemical   d. medical

4. The man needs some _____ treatment at once.
   a. deaf   b. medical   c. lively   d. active

5. She was really upset about the _____ of her grandmother.
   a. nutrition   b. cause   c. growth   d. death

E **Read the passage. Then, write T for true or F for false.**

Janet had an **appointment** to see the doctor. She thought she had a **physical** problem. "What's the matter with me, Dr. Nelson?" she asked. "Do I have **cancer**?" Dr. Nelson said, "Please **relax**, Janet. You don't have **cancer**. However, you have a **nutrition** problem."

"What do you mean?" she asked. "You eat too much junk food," Dr. Nelson answered. "The junk food is **harming** your body. Your body cannot **digest** all of that sugar. So it is **causing** problems with your body's **functions**." Janet was surprised. "Will I **recover**?" she asked. "Of course. You don't even need **drugs**. Just start eating food with lots of **nutrition**. And stop eating so much chocolate, candy, and ice cream. You will feel **lively** and be **active** again in no time."

1. Janet's doctor tells her she has cancer. _____

2. The doctor says Janet eats too much junk food. _____

3. Sugar is causing problems in Janet's body. _____

4. Janet's doctor gives her some drugs to take. _____

1 advertise
[ǽdvərtàiz]
n. advertisement

v. to tell people about a product so that they will buy it
(syn) promote
advertise a product
→ The company **advertises** its products online.

2 allowance
[əláuəns]
v. allow

n. money given to a person regularly   (syn) pocket money
weekly allowance
→ Jane's weekly **allowance** is $10.

3 benefit
[bénifit]

n. something good that provides an advantage   (ant) harm
v. to do good or to help
provide a benefit → Reading books can provide many **benefits**.
benefit others → Her good work **benefits** others.

4 bet
[bet]
bet - bet - bet

n. the act of risking money on an event
v. to risk money on an event
lose a bet → Dave lost his **bet** with Chris.
bet on something → Patrick will **bet** on the horse race.

5 billion
[bíljən]

n. 1,000,000,000; one thousand million
billion dollars
→ The bridge cost two **billion** dollars to build.

6 budget
[bʌ́dʒit]

n. the amount of money a person or group can spend
monthly budget
→ He sometimes goes over his monthly **budget**.

7 business
[bíznəs]

n. the work of buying or selling products or services for money   (syn) trade
computer business
→ Lisa owns a successful computer **business**.

8 capital
[kǽpitəl]

n. money that is invested or used to start a business
raise capital
→ The boss tried hard to raise more **capital**.

9 charge
[tʃɑːrdʒ]

v. to ask for a price or fee
n. a cost   (syn) expense
charge tax → The government **charges** tax on many things.
extra charge → There is an extra **charge** for drinks.

10 expense
[ikspéns]

n. an amount of money used to buy or do something
(syn) payment
living expense
→ Living **expenses** in New York are very high.

11 gain
[ɡein]

v. to get something   (syn) receive   (ant) lose
gain knowledge
→ You can **gain** knowledge by reading books.

12 income
[ínkʌm]

n. the money a person or company makes   (syn) salary
annual income
→ Her annual **income** goes up each year.

13 opportunity
[ɑ̀pərtjúːnəti]

n. a good chance to succeed
have an opportunity
→ She has an **opportunity** to win the game.

14 period
[pí(ː)əriəd]

n. a specific amount of time
short period
→ She learned the piano for a short **period** of time.

15 poverty
[pɑ́vərti]
adj. poor

n. the state of having little or no money   (ant) wealth
live in poverty
→ Many people in this country live in **poverty**.

16 quarter
[kwɔ́ːrtər]

n. one of four equal parts of something
first quarter
→ The first **quarter** of the year is from January to March.

17 resource
[ríːsɔ̀ːrs]

n. useful things that a country or person has
valuable resource
→ Gold is a valuable **resource** for people.

18 salary
[sǽləri]

n. money a person is paid regularly for work   (syn) pay
high salary
→ Most doctors receive high **salaries**.

19 shopkeeper
[ʃɑ́pkìːpər]

n. a person who runs or owns a small store
friendly shopkeeper
→ Customers like the friendly **shopkeeper**.

20 support
[səpɔ́ːrt]

v. to hold up or take care of
n. the act of holding up or taking care of
support one's family   → Mr. Taylor tries hard to **support** his family.
financial support   → Mark receives financial **support** from his parents.

A **Match the words with their definitions.**

1. billion   •   • a. useful things that a country or person has

2. budget   •   • b. a good chance to succeed

3. benefit   •   • c. an amount of money used to buy or do something

4. expense   •   • d. a specific amount of time

5. resource   •   • e. to do good or to help

6. opportunity •   • f. the amount of money a person or group can spend

7. quarter   •   • g. one of four equal parts of something

8. period   •   • h. one thousand million

B **Circle the two words in each group that have the same meaning.**

1. a. salary   b. resource   c. charge   d. expense

2. a. salary   b. business   c. opportunity   d. pay

3. a. gain   b. receive   c. benefit   d. period

4. a. bet   b. promote   c. advertise   d. support

C **Circle the words that best fit the sentences.**

1. The company does not have enough capital | salary to build a factory.

2. Joe spent his weekly period | allowance on candy at the store.

3. Mr. Johnson works hard to support | benefit his wife and children.

4. Millions of people around the world live in quarter | poverty .

5. He gained | bet a lot of experience at his job.

6. The restaurant advertised | charged the man for two meals by mistake.

D Choose the correct words to complete the sentences.

1. Doug's _____ increases at his job every year.

    a. period   b. capital   c. income   d. resource

2. Some people like to _____ on the results of sporting events.

    a. bet   b. charge   c. support   d. gain

3. The store often _____ on TV and the Internet.

    a. charges   b. advertises   c. benefits   d. gains

4. My mother works as a _____ at a small grocery store.

    a. salary   b. business   c. quarter   d. shopkeeper

5. Alice works in the automobile _____.

    a. expense   b. budget   c. business   d. period

E Read the passage. Then, fill in the blanks.

There are **billions** of people in the world today. Many of them live in **poverty**. However, a lot of those people have **opportunities** to improve their lives. If they take advantage of these **opportunities**, they can **benefit** greatly.

For instance, some people work difficult jobs for long **periods** of time. Their **salaries** may be small, but they can keep most of their **income**. Later, they may open their own small **businesses**. Some of these people become **shopkeepers**. They can do **business** with customers and **gain** more **capital**. They may start to **advertise** their services on television or in the newspaper. They can then **benefit** by getting more customers. Over time, the amount of **resources** these people have increases, so their lives improve.

1. Many people in the world live in _____.

2. Some people can _____ by taking advantage of opportunities.

3. Some people open business and become _____.

4. Shops may get more customers when people _____ their services.

1	**abroad** [əbrɔ́:d]	*adv.* in or to a foreign country travel abroad ➜ Janet likes to travel **abroad** every year.
2	**available** [əvéiləbl]	*adj.* ready to be used; not too busy to do something available resource ➜ There are not enough **available** resources now. available for ➜ Mr. White is **available** for dinner tonight.
3	**border** [bɔ́:rdər]	*n.* the line separating two countries, states, etc. cross the border ➜ You need a passport to cross the **border**.
4	**castle** [kǽsl]	*n.* a strong home with walls around it syn palace build a castle ➜ The knight built a **castle** on top of the hill.
5	**coast** [koust]	*n.* the land by the sea syn shore on the coast ➜ We have a beautiful house on the **coast**.
6	**comfort** [kʌ́mfərt] *adj.* comfortable	*v.* to make someone feel better *n.* a feeling of relief or happiness syn ease comfort someone ➜ The music **comforted** the crying baby. in comfort ➜ She lives in **comfort** on an island.
7	**cost** [kɔ(:)st]	*n.* the amount of money needed to pay for something syn price *v.* to require payment for something low cost ➜ Her watch was on sale for a low **cost**. cost a lot ➜ It **costs** a lot to visit the amusement park.
8	**cultural** [kʌ́ltʃərəl] *n.* culture	*adj.* relating to a particular society, customs, and art cultural difference ➜ The two countries have some **cultural** differences.
9	**encounter** [inkáuntər]	*v.* to meet a person, often by accident; to experience something encounter someone ➜ I **encountered** my old friend at the store. encounter a problem ➜ He **encountered** a problem at work.
10	**fortunate** [fɔ́:rtʃənət] *adv.* fortunately	*adj.* having or bringing good luck syn lucky ant unlucky fortunate person ➜ Leslie is such a **fortunate** person.

11 journey
[dʒə́ːrni]

n. a long trip to a distant place

make a journey

→ She makes a **journey** abroad once a year

12 local
[lóukəl]

adj. related to the area that someone lives in

local market

→ The vegetables at the **local** market are fresh.

13 native
[néitiv]

adj. relating to the place a person was born

native language

→ Ivan's **native** language is Russian.

14 nearby
[niərbái]

adj./adv. not far away   (syn) close   (ant) distant

nearby city → We visited a **nearby** city last weekend.

live nearby → My grandparents live **nearby**.

15 observe
[əbzə́ːrv]

v. to see or notice; to watch carefully   (ant) ignore

observe an accident → He **observed** an accident outside the school.

observe the stars → Kate likes to **observe** the stars at night.

16 passenger
[pǽsindʒər]

n. a person riding in a vehicle

safety of passengers

→ The safety of **passengers** is very important.

17 preserve
[prizə́ːrv]

v. to keep alive or safe   (syn) save

preserve nature

→ It is important to **preserve** nature for the future.

18 remain
[riméin]

v. to stay in the same place or condition   (ant) leave

remain home

→ I decided to **remain** home last weekend.

19 sightseeing
[sáitsìːiŋ]

n. the act of visiting places of interest

go sightseeing

→ They will go **sightseeing** in Paris tomorrow.

20 village
[vílidʒ]

n. a small town in a rural area

move to a village

→ His family moved to a **village** to enjoy country life.

A Circle the correct definitions for the given words.

1. encounter

a. to see or notice

b. to keep alive or safe

c. to experience something

d. to make someone feel better

2. local

a. having or bringing good luck

b. related to the area that someone lives in

c. in or to a foreign country

d. ready to be used

3. native

a. not too busy to do something

b. having or bringing good luck

c. not far away

d. relating to the place a person was born

4. passenger

a. a long trip to a distant place

b. a feeling of relief or happiness

c. a person riding in a vehicle

d. the land by the sea

B Write S for synonym or A for antonym next to each pair of words.

1. _____ coast – shore

2. _____ remain – leave

3. _____ nearby – distant

4. _____ observe – ignore

5. _____ castle – palace

6. _____ preserve – save

C Circle the words that best fit the sentences.

1. We plan to go passenger | sightseeing in Rome next week.

2. You are fortunate | local to be okay after the accident.

3. Only a few people live in the journey | village in the countryside.

4. He lives on the cost | border of the two countries.

5. Please remain | preserve in your seats for a few minutes.

6. Mr. Jefferson is not available | cultural to take your call now.

D Choose the correct words to complete the sentences.

1. He has lived in _____ since he won the lottery.

    a. comfort   b. sightseeing   c. passenger   d. cost

2. Janet will travel _____ to Europe during winter.

    a. available   b. cultural   c. abroad   d. native

3. Columbus made a long _____ across the ocean.

    a. castle   b. journey   c. border   d. village

4. It _____ a lot of money to join that gym.

    a. remains   b. costs   c. preserves   d. observes

5. There are many items of _____ importance at the museum.

    a. nearby   b. available   c. fortunate   d. cultural

E Read the passage. Then, write T for true or F for false.

 These days, people in countries around the world love to travel **abroad**. Some people simply enjoy **sightseeing**. They visit large cities or the **coast** and go to **nearby** places of **cultural** interest. These include museums, galleries, and **castles**. They like to **remain** in crowded places. They travel in **comfort** and stay at nice hotels. They believe they are very **fortunate** because they can travel **abroad**.

Other people take different kinds of trips **abroad**. They like to visit **villages** in the countryside. There, they can **encounter native** citizens. They talk with **local** residents and **observe** their everyday lives. For these travelers, learning firsthand about other cultures is very important. They do not care about the **costs** of their trips. They just want to have a wonderful time.

1. Some people like to go sightseeing in large cities. _____

2. Some people stay at nice hotels and travel in comfort. _____

3. Some people encounter native citizens in castles. _____

4. It is important for some travelers to learn about other cultures. _____

A Choose and write the correct words for the definitions.

hunger	greenhouse	chemical	curious
typhoon	village	shock	bet

1. eager to know about something ➡ _____

2. the need or desire for food ➡ _____

3. a small town in a rural area ➡ _____

4. a building used to grow plants in any season ➡ _____

5. to surprise or upset a person ➡ _____

6. the act of risking money on an event ➡ _____

7. a violent tropical storm ➡ _____

8. a material produced or used in chemistry ➡ _____

B Circle the words that are the most similar to the underlined words.

1. Janet is <u>active</u> and always likes to do things.

    a. medical   b. chemical   c. lively   d. deaf

2. The king built a new <u>palace</u> in another city.

    a. journey   b. passenger   c. sightseeing   d. castle

3. The students are <u>nervous</u> about the performance on stage.

    a. useless   b. foolish   c. gentle   d. anxious

4. Your <u>vision</u> will improve if you wear contact lenses.

    a. liquid   b. sight   c. horizon   d. climate

5. What is the <u>pay</u> for the job?

    a. salary   b. business   c. poverty   d. period

C Choose the correct forms of the words to complete the sentences.

1. We all enjoyed the scene | scenery at the national park.

2. I hope you can recover | recovery from your sickness.

3. John is often cheer | cheerful and talks to everyone.

4. She was fortunate | fortunately not to get hurt in the accident.

5. Justin receives an allowance | allow from his parents every Saturday.

D Complete the sentences with the words in the box.

1. This broken machine is _____ to us.

2. The boss gave the team a big _____ for the project.

3. We plan to _____ the events up close.

4. With proper _____, you can improve your health.

5. There are many _____ on trees in April.

> nutrition
>
> useless
>
> blossoms
>
> observe
>
> budget

E Write the correct phrases in the blanks.

| digest food | unhappy life | has an opportunity |
| valuable resources | strange creature | cultural differences |

1. I saw a _____ living in the swamp.

2. You need to give your stomach time to _____.

3. _____ like oil and coal are in this land.

4. It is sad that Fred has such an _____.

5. You should learn some _____ before traveling.

6. Chris _____ to make a lot of money.

F **Circle the mistakes. Then, write the correct sentences.**

1. I have an appoint with the dentist tomorrow.

   ➡ _____

2. The factories pollution the air too much.

   ➡ _____

3. She sleeps in comfortable on a soft bed.

   ➡ _____

4. Everyone thinks Tim has a great personal.

   ➡ _____

5. That man leads a life of poor.

   ➡ _____

G **Complete the crossword puzzle.**

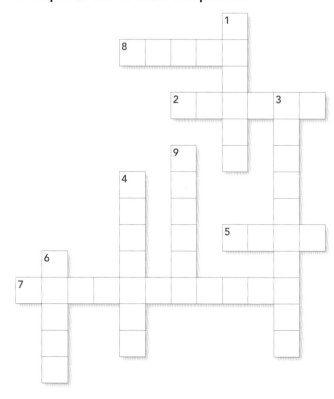

Across

2. to annoy someone

5. to get something

7. an area with fields away from cities

8. to make something happen

Down

1. to agree to a solution

3. a test done to try to learn something new

4. one of four equal parts of something

6. the land by the sea

9. not far away

H **Read the passage. Then, answer the questions below.**

A New Type of Treatment

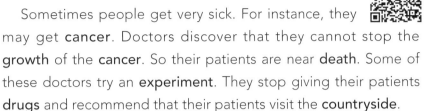

Sometimes people get very sick. For instance, they may get **cancer**. Doctors discover that they cannot stop the **growth** of the **cancer**. So their patients are near **death**. Some of these doctors try an **experiment**. They stop giving their patients **drugs** and recommend that their patients visit the **countryside**.

The **atmosphere** there is different. There is beautiful **scenery**. Their patients can enjoy a nice **climate**. They **encounter** and **observe** wild animals and beautiful **blossoms**, too. The land is peaceful, so their patients are filled with **happiness**.

In some cases, the doctors are **shocked**. Being in the **countryside** provides **benefits** for their patients. Some of them begin to **recover**. They have an **opportunity** to live full lives again. This method does not work for everyone. But all of the patients become more **cheerful** and lose their feelings of **anger**.

1. What is the passage mainly about?

   a. people with cancer

   b. the atmosphere in spring

   c. a way doctors treat some patients

   d. methods people use to become happy

2. Where do doctors tell some patients to go?

   a. to big cities

   b. to the countryside

   c. to another country

   d. to their hometowns

3. What happens to some patients after being in the countryside?

   a. They become sicker.

   b. They find new doctors.

   c. They return to the hospital.

   d. They begin to recover.

4. What do doctors stop doing for some patients?

   ➡ _____

5. What happens to all of the patients after being in the countryside?

   ➡ _____

31

Unit 06 | Word List

1 admire
[ədmáiər]

v. to like or praise someone or something   (syn) respect   (ant) dislike
admire someone
→ Chris **admires** his father for several reasons.

2 apologize
[əpálədʒàiz]
n. apology

v. to say that one is sorry
apologize sincerely
→ You should **apologize** sincerely to him.

3 argue
[á:rgju:]
n. argument

v. to state why one is for or against something
argue for something
→ The lawyer is **arguing** for the death penalty.

4 awkward
[ɔ́:kwərd]

adj. embarrassing and difficult to deal with   (ant) comfortable
awkward comment
→ Nobody responded to Tim's **awkward** comment.

5 behave
[bihéiv]
n. behavior

v. to act in a certain way, often properly
behave oneself
→ Please **behave** yourself at school.

6 blame
[bleim]

v. to find a person at fault   (ant) praise
blame somebody
→ Don't **blame** me for the accident.

7 community
[kəmjú:nəti]

n. a group of people who live in the same area
local community
→ Jane is active in the local **community**.

8 conversation
[kànvərséiʃən]

n. an informal talk between people   (syn) chat
have a conversation
→ They had a **conversation** about sports.

9 disagree
[dìsəgrí:]
n. disagreement

v. to have a different opinion   (ant) agree
disagree with
→ Peter **disagreed** with Dave about the problem.

10 frankly
[frǽŋkli]

adv. in an honest or direct manner   (syn) honestly
frankly speaking
→ **Frankly** speaking, I do not care about it.

11 generous
[dʒénərəs]

adj. giving or sharing   (ant) selfish

generous man

→ Mr. Thompson is a very **generous** man.

12 ignore
[ignɔ́ːr]

v. not to listen to or follow someone

ignore one's advice

→ Please do not **ignore** my advice.

13 inspire
[inspáiər]

n. inspiration

v. to influence people in a positive way   (syn) encourage

inspire someone

→ Matt **inspired** his friends to study hard.

14 lifetime
[láiftàim]

n. the period when something lives

once in a lifetime

→ Haley's Comet comes once in a **lifetime**.

15 marry
[mǽri]

n. marriage

v. to become the husband or wife of someone

marry someone

→ Jim finally **married** his girlfriend last year.

16 passion
[pǽʃən]

n. a strong feeling of love or hate

passion for

→ Greg has a real **passion** for classical music.

17 professional
[prəféʃənəl]

adj. relating to work that needs special training or skill

professional golfer

→ He wants to become a **professional** golfer.

18 relationship
[riléiʃənʃip]

n. a connection between people

start a relationship

→ They started their **relationship** ten years ago.

19 responsible
[rispánsəbl]

adj. having to do something or take care of somebody

be responsible → John is **responsible** and always does his work.

responsible for → The teacher is **responsible** for the students.

20 worried
[wʌ́ːrid]

adj. concerned about something   (syn) anxious

worried about

→ She is **worried** about her grade.

A **Circle the words that fit the definitions.**

1. a group of people who live in the same area

    a. conversation   b. community   c. passion   d. lifetime

2. relating to work that needs special training or skill

    a. professional   b. worried   c. generous   d. responsible

3. not to listen to or follow someone

    a. blame   b. admire   c. apologize   d. ignore

4. embarrassing and difficult to deal with

    a. responsible   b. awkward   c. frankly   d. worried

5. a connection between people

    a. passion   b. lifetime   c. relationship   d. conversation

B **Choose and write the correct words for the blanks.**

blame	frankly	conversation	awkward	disagree	admire

1. respect = _____

2. praise ≠ _____

3. honestly = _____

4. agree ≠ _____

5. chat = _____

6. comfortable ≠ _____

C **Circle the words that best fit the sentences.**

1. She will marry | admire her boyfriend this Saturday.

2. John ignores | inspires people to do their best.

3. You must behave | disagree well when you are at school.

4. They went on the trip of a lifetime | conversation .

5. She is awkward | generous and loves to share with others.

6. I am worried | professional that I wrote the wrong answer on the test.

D Choose the correct words to complete the sentences.

1. _____, George is the hardest worker at the company.

   a. Generous   b. Frankly   c. Worried   d. Awkward

2. He has a _____ for working in his garden every summer.

   a. community   b. lifetime   c. relationship   d. passion

3. Please do not _____ with your mother so much.

   a. argue   b. admire   c. behave   d. marry

4. Who is _____ for taking out the garbage?

   a. awkward   b. professional   c. responsible   d. worried

5. She _____ for yelling at her father.

   a. married   b. ignored   c. inspired   d. apologized

E Read the passage. Then, fill in the blanks.

A **community** is a group of people who live closely together. Many people live in the same **community** for their entire **lifetimes**. A **community** is made of all kinds of people. Some are **generous** while others are selfish. Some have a **passion** for various activities while others just enjoy having simple **conversations** with their neighbors.

People in a **community** have various **relationships** with one another. Sometimes people might **marry** others living in their **community**. On the other hand, some neighbors **argue** a lot. They might **blame** their neighbors for various problems. They **behave** badly toward one another and never **apologize**. But some people **inspire** others. This causes other people to **admire** them. Clearly, there are all kinds of people who live together in a **community**.

1. There are many kinds of people in a _____.

2. Some people like to have simple _____ with others.

3. Some neighbors _____ with other people a lot.

4. Some people inspire others, so people _____ them.

35

1 achieve
[ətʃíːv]

v. to do something well or successfully (ant) fail
achieve one's goal
→ Sue **achieved** her goal of becoming a lawyer.

2 average
[ǽvəridʒ]

adj. referring to a typical amount, rate, number, etc. (syn) normal
average height
→ Tina is **average** height for a ten-year-old.

3 cheat
[tʃiːt]

v. to act in a dishonest way (syn) trick
cheat on a test
→ Susan was punished for **cheating** on the test.

4 clever
[klévər]

adj. smart (syn) intelligent (ant) stupid
clever child
→ The **clever** child solved the mystery.

5 compete
[kəmpíːt]
n. competition

v. to try to do better than others (syn) contest
compete for
→ People **compete** for gold medals at the Olympics.

6 concentrate
[kánsəntrèit]
n. concentration

v. to focus on or think about something very much
concentrate on
→ You should **concentrate** on the teacher.

7 excellent
[éksələnt]

adj. very good (ant) terrible
excellent grade
→ Dave got an **excellent** grade on the final exam.

8 genius
[dʒíːnjəs]

n. a very smart person (ant) fool
genius at
→ Einstein was a **genius** at physics.

9 information
[ìnfərméiʃən]
v. inform

n. knowledge or facts
information age
→ We are living in an **information** age.

10 progress
[prəgrés][prágres]

v. to move forward or to develop (syn) improve
n. movement forward or the process of development
progress in → Leah is **progressing** in her piano lessons.
in progress → The game is in **progress** now.

11 pronounce
[prənáuns]
n. pronunciation

v. to say the sound of a word or letter
pronounce a word
→ How do you **pronounce** this word?

12 purpose
[pɔ́ːrpəs]

n. the reason something exists
on purpose
→ The player missed the ball on **purpose**.

13 research
[rísɜːrtʃ]
n. researcher

v. to study something carefully
n. a careful study of something
research a topic → Why do you **research** the topic?
do research → I will do some **research** on earthquakes.

14 review
[rivjúː]

v. to go over something again
review one's notes
→ **Review** your notes before the test.

15 solution
[səljúːʃən]
v. solve

n. an explanation or answer   syn result
find a solution
→ Please find a **solution** to this problem.

16 subtract
[səbtrǽkt]

v. to take one number away from another   ant add
subtract a number
→ You should **subtract** the smaller number from the larger number.

17 system
[sístəm]

n. a combination of things to create a whole
security system
→ We should check the security **system** in the building.

18 teenager
[tíːnèidʒər]

n. a person between the ages of 13 and 19
become a teenager
→ Fran is so excited to become a **teenager**.

19 textbook
[tékstbùk]

n. a book used in a classroom
read a textbook
→ Read the **textbook** before the next class.

20 total
[tóutl]
adv. totally

n. a complete amount
adj. relating to the whole of something
in total → You owe twenty dollars in **total**.
total cost → The **total** cost is more than ten dollars.

37

A Match the words with their definitions.

1. total •   • a. to study something carefully

2. teenager •   • b. to move forward or to develop

3. average •   • c. a complete amount

4. research •   • d. referring to a typical amount, rate, number, etc.

5. genius •   • e. a combination of things to create a whole

6. progress •   • f. a very smart person

7. system •   • g. a person between the ages of 13 and 19

8. achieve •   • h. to do something well or successfully

B Circle the two words in each group that have the same meaning.

1. a. compete   b. achieve   c. contest   d. cheat

2. a. information   b. result   c. purpose   d. solution

3. a. average   b. total   c. intelligent   d. clever

4. a. progress   b. improve   c. concentrate   d. subtract

C Circle the words that best fit the sentences.

1. Please turn to page 17 in your system | textbook .

2. You need to compete | review your paper at once.

3. The students will learn to subtract | pronounce in math class.

4. You should never achieve | cheat when you play a game.

5. We need more information | purpose to find the answer.

6. The play was so total | excellent that we will see it again tomorrow.

D **Choose the correct words to complete the sentences.**

1. He knows how to _____ English words correctly.

   a. pronounce   b. subtract   c. progress   d. compete

2. She spent a _____ of five hours working on the essay.

   a. genius   b. teenager   c. total   d. textbook

3. The _____ grade on the test was 85.

   a. clever   b. average   c. solution   d. system

4. We do not know the _____ of that tool over there.

   a. research   b. genius   c. teenager   d. purpose

5. You must _____ very hard to think of the right answer.

   a. concentrate   b. cheat   c. achieve   d. subtract

E **Read the passage. Then, write T for true or F for false.**

 Frank and Scott are **teenagers**. They are **average** students, so their grades are neither high nor low. One day, Frank decides to **achieve** more. He knows he is not a **genius**. However, he is still **clever**. So he wants to get better grades. He is not sure how to do that.

    He asks Scott what to do. Scott says, "You should **cheat** to get higher grades." Frank says, "That's not right, Scott." Frank decides not to **cheat**. Instead, he starts to **concentrate** more in class. He also **reviews** his notes and does **research** after class. Finally, he decides to read the **textbook** more often. Frank's ideas are all **excellent**. He begins to **progress** in his classes. By the end of the semester, he is an A student.

1. Frank and Scott are the best students.   _____

2. Frank is clever but not a genius.   _____

3. Scott tells Frank to cheat in class to get better grades.   _____

4. Scott concentrates hard in class and becomes an A student.   _____

1	**architect** [ɑ́ːrkitèkt] *n.* architecture	*n.* a person who designs buildings famous architect → This church was built by a famous **architect**.	
2	**astronaut** [ǽstrənɔ̀ːt]	*n.* a person who lives or works in space NASA astronaut → Neil Armstrong was a NASA **astronaut**.	
3	**athlete** [ǽθliːt]	*n.* a person who plays and competes in a sport train an athlete → The coach has trained many Olympic **athletes**.	
4	**author** [ɔ́ːθər]	*n.* a person who writes books, articles, etc. *(syn)* writer famous author → The novel made him a famous **author**.	
5	**compose** [kəmpóuz] *n.* composer	*v.* to make or form something; to write music *(ant)* destroy compose a group → Ten men **compose** the group. compose music → Mozart **composed** very much beautiful music.	
6	**conductor** [kəndʌ́ktər]	*n.* someone who directs the musicians in an orchestra guest conductor → Today's guest **conductor** is Mr. Willis.	
7	**dedication** [dèdikéiʃən]	*n.* the hard work and effort a person spends great dedication → She has great **dedication** toward her family.	
8	**diligent** [dílidʒənt]	*adj.* constantly trying to do something *(ant)* lazy diligent student → Harry is the most **diligent** student in the class.	
9	**engineer** [èndʒiníər]	*n.* a person trained to use engines or machines mechanical engineer → My father works as a mechanical **engineer**.	
10	**equipment** [ikwípmənt]	*n.* anything kept or used for a certain purpose *(syn)* tool carry equipment → Firefighters carry lots of **equipment** to burning buildings.	

11 focus
[fóukəs]

v. to give attention to one thing   (syn) concentrate
focus on
→ You should **focus** on studying while in class.

12 influence
[ínfluəns]

v. to have a big effect on something   (syn) affect
n. the act of affecting others
influence someone → Mr. Patterson **influenced** people a lot.
big influence → My parents have a big **influence** on me.

13 intelligent
[intélidʒənt]

adj. very smart   (syn) clever   (ant) stupid
intelligent solution
→ Who can suggest an **intelligent** solution to the problem?

14 invent
[invént]

n. invention

v. to make something new   (syn) create
invent a story
→ Shakespeare was great at **inventing** stories.

15 manage
[mǽnidʒ]

n. manager

v. to run or be in charge of something
manage a hotel
→ It's difficult to **manage** a big hotel.

16 newspaper
[njúːzpèipər]

n. a paper issued regularly that has news stories
read the newspaper
→ My father reads the **newspaper** every day.

17 organize
[ɔ́ːrgənàiz]

n. organization

v. to prepare an activity or event; to put things into order
organize a meeting → She is busy **organizing** a meeting.
organize papers → Please **organize** the papers on your desk.

18 performance
[pərfɔ́ːrməns]

v. perform

n. a type of entertainment people watch
put on a performance
→ The group put on a **performance** of *Hamlet*.

19 role
[roul]

n. a part that an actor plays; the function that someone has
play a role → He will play the **role** of Romeo.
important role → Tim has an important **role** on the team.

20 successful
[səksésfəl]

n. success

adj. achieving one's goal   (ant) failed
successful life
→ Everyone wants to live a **successful** life.

A   **Circle the words that fit the definitions.**

1. a part that an actor plays

a. influence   b. dedication   c. newspaper   d. role

2. to run or be in charge of something

a. manage   b. compose   c. invent   d. focus

3. someone who directs the musicians in an orchestra

a. conductor   b. architect   c. athlete   d. astronaut

4. anything kept or used for a certain purpose

a. dedication   b. performance   c. equipment   d. influence

5. a person who plays and competes in a sport

a. engineer   b. athlete   c. author   d. architect

B   **Circle the two words in each group that are opposites.**

1. a. intelligent   b. manage   c. invent   d. stupid

2. a. dedication   b. failed   c. successful   d. role

3. a. compose   b. destroy   c. focus   d. influence

4. a. engineer   b. equipment   c. lazy   d. diligent

C   **Circle the words that best fit the sentences.**

1. Lucy will help organize | focus the school picnic.

2. Her father is an astronaut | architect who designs homes.

3. He is trying to manage | invent a flying car.

4. She is a reporter for the local role | newspaper .

5. It takes a lot of dedication | performance to learn a musical instrument.

6. The teacher was a good influence | equipment on her students.

D Choose the correct words to complete the sentences.

1. You must _____ hard when you are taking a test.

   a. manage   b. invent   c. compose   d. focus

2. Everyone clapped loudly when the _____ ended.

   a. performance   b. equipment   c. athlete   d. conductor

3. The _____ will visit the moon next year.

   a. influence   b. astronaut   c. dedication   d. role

4. The _____ is helping design the new bridge.

   a. newspaper   b. role   c. equipment   d. engineer

5. The _____ of the *Harry Potter* series is J. K. Rowling.

   a. engineer   b. architect   c. author   d. astronaut

E **Read the passage. Then, fill in the blanks.**

 After finishing high school, many young people go to college. There, they can **focus** on certain subjects. Some want to be **engineers**, so they study math and science. Then, they can try to **invent** things in the future. Others want to be **authors**, so they **focus** on writing classes. Some of them write for the school **newspaper**, too. And others want to be **architects**, **conductors**, and even **athletes**. They all study different subjects.

   College students must be **diligent** and have **dedication**. They need to **focus** on their lessons and do their homework. Then, they can do well in their classes and be **successful**. Students must **manage** their time well, too. Then, they will do well at school. If they are **successful**, they can graduate and find great jobs.

1. Students _____ on different subjects in college.

2. Some students who want to be authors write for the school _____.

3. Students must be _____ and have dedication at college.

4. _____ students can graduate and get good jobs.

1	**animation** [æniméiʃən]	*n.* a cartoon that uses drawings to create motion *syn* comic make an animation → Disney made an **animation** about the story.
2	**attractive** [ətrǽktiv] *v.* attract	*adj.* pleasing and nice looking *ant* ugly attractive woman → Wendy is a very **attractive** woman.
3	**audience** [ɔ́:diəns]	*n.* a group of people watching a movie, game, etc. bow to the audience → At the end, the actors bowed to the **audience**.
4	**background** [bǽkgràund]	*n.* the rear part of a scene, painting, etc. dark background → The painting has a dark **background**.
5	**cancel** [kǽnsəl]	*v.* to decide not to hold a planned event *syn* stop cancel a picnic → They **canceled** the picnic because of the rain.
6	**celebration** [sèlibréiʃən] *v.* celebrate	*n.* a party or festival for a special day have a celebration → We have a **celebration** on New Year's Day.
7	**choir** [kwáiər]	*n.* a group of singers, often in a church sing in a choir → Mr. Roberts sings in the **choir** at his church.
8	**decorate** [dékərèit] *n.* decoration	*v.* to make a place look nicer decorate a room → We will **decorate** the room for the party.
9	**exhibit** [igzíbit] *n.* exhibition	*v.* to show something like art *syn* display *n.* a special show exhibit a painting → The gallery **exhibits** many paintings. museum exhibit → We were excited to see the museum **exhibit**.
10	**hobby** [hάbi]	*n.* an activity a person does for fun or to relax *syn* pastime as a hobby → My mother draws pictures as a **hobby**.

11 mystery
[místəri]
adj. mysterious

n. something secret or unknown
unsolved mystery
→ Pyramids are an unsolved **mystery**.

12 novel
[návəl]

n. a long written work of fiction
read a novel
→ People usually read **novels** for fun.

13 pretend
[priténd]

v. to act like something is real   (syn) imagine
pretend to
→ Jane is just **pretending** to be asleep.

14 probably
[prábəbli]

adv. likely to happen   (syn) perhaps
probably win
→ The team will **probably** win the game.

15 publish
[pábliʃ]

v. to print a book, newspaper, magazine, etc.
publish a book
→ The author has **published** more than ten books.

16 realistic
[rì(:)əlístik]
n. reality

adj. relating to things as they actually are   (syn) practical
realistic movie
→ That documentary is a **realistic** movie.

17 script
[skript]

n. the written text of a play, movie, speech, etc.
write a script
→ He writes movie **scripts** for a living.

18 situation
[sìtʃuéiʃən]

n. a current condition   (syn) state
bad situation
→ How did you overcome your bad **situation**?

19 technology
[teknálədʒi]

n. knowledge of machines, engineering, and science
modern technology
→ Modern **technology** has changed our lives a lot.

20 vivid
[vívid]

adj. clear, lively, or bright   (ant) dull
vivid blue
→ The color of the sky in fall is **vivid** blue.

A **Circle the correct definitions for the given words.**

1. situation

   a. a special show

   b. a current condition

   c. a party or festival for a special day

   d. the rear part of a scene, painting, etc.

2. publish

   a. to act like something is real

   b. to make a place look nicer

   c. to show something like art

   d. to print a book, newspaper, magazine, etc.

3. mystery

   a. something secret or unknown

   b. a group of singers, often in a church

   c. a long written work of fiction

   d. a special show

4. attractive

   a. likely to happen

   b. clear, lively, or bright

   c. pleasing and nice looking

   d. relating to things as they actually are

B **Circle the two words in each group that have the same meaning.**

1. a. pretend   b. cancel   c. imagine   d. exhibit

2. a. script   b. comic   c. hobby   d. animation

3. a. publish   b. decorate   c. perhaps   d. probably

4. a. practical   b. realistic   c. vivid   d. attractive

C **Circle the words that best fit the sentences.**

1. The museum will have an audience | exhibit on art next week.

2. I want to read the script | celebration for that movie.

3. Let's pretend | decorate the room for the Christmas party.

4. Every member of the choir | novel can sing very well.

5. The background colors of the painting are quite vivid | probably .

6. Thanks to hobby | technology , humans have gone to the moon.

D **Choose the correct words to complete the sentences.**

1. Everyone in the _____ clapped for the actors.
    a. audience   b. hobby   c. technology   d. mystery

2. She tries to read at least one _____ each week.
    a. choir   b. exhibit   c. novel   d. situation

3. We will have a _____ on the last day of school.
    a. celebration   b. background   c. situation   d. script

4. I would like to _____ my plane reservation.
    a. pretend   b. cancel   c. publish   d. decorate

5. His _____ is collecting coins from other countries.
    a. exhibit   b. animation   c. mystery   d. hobby

E **Read the passage. Then, write T for true or F for false.**

The students at Central High School all have **hobbies**. They are fun activities that people do in their free time. Jessica likes to **decorate** things. Her bedroom looks really **attractive** because of all the decorations. She always helps **decorate** the classroom for **celebrations** like birthday parties. Tom loves **technology**. His **hobby** is trying to create different kinds of machines. Susan and Greg enjoy **animation**. They write **scripts** and then create short **animations**. They will show one to an **audience** this weekend.

David's **hobby** is reading **novels**. He likes to read mysterious stories these days. So thrillers are his favorite **novels** now. Finally, Anna really likes art. Her **hobby** is painting **realistic** art. She uses **vivid** colors in her paintings. She will **probably** become an artist in the future.

1. Jessica decorates her bedroom and the classroom. _____

2. Tom likes to write scripts and make animations. _____

3. David's hobby is writing novels. _____

4. Anna uses vivid colors to paint realistic art. _____

1	**aim**
	[eim]
		n. the goal of doing something (syn) purpose
		v. to point a gun at something
		   one's aim → His **aim** is to get a good grade.
		   aim a gun → The soldier **aimed** the gun at the enemy.

2	**arrow**
	[ǽrou]
		n. a long, thin weapon which is sharp and pointed at one end
		   bow and arrow
		   → John likes to go hunting with a bow and **arrow**.

3	**attack**
	[ətǽk]
		v. to try to hurt or kill someone (syn) invade (ant) defend
		   attack an enemy
		   → The army **attacked** the enemy at night.

4	**campaign**
	[kæmpéin]
		n. a series of military, social, or political actions
		   election campaign
		   → He is preparing for an election **campaign**.

5	**capture**
	[kǽptʃər]
		v. to catch and hold a person or animal (syn) arrest (ant) release
		   capture a prisoner
		   → The police **captured** several prisoners.

6	**command**
	[kəmǽnd]
	n. commander
		v. to order others
		n. an official order
		   command an army → Alexander **commanded** a powerful army.
		   obey a command → We must obey the captain's **command**.

7	**damage**
	[dǽmidʒ]
		v. to cause harm to someone or something
		n. harm or injury
		   damage one's car → I **damaged** my car in the crash.
		   suffer damage → She suffered **damage** to her body.

8	**destroy**
	[distrɔ́i]
		v. to kill, defeat, or damage (ant) build
		   destroy a building
		   → The bomb **destroyed** the building.

9	**empire**
	[émpaiər]
	n. emperor
		n. a group of nations ruled by an emperor
		   Roman Empire
		   → The Roman **Empire** once ruled most of Europe.

10	**guard**
	[gɑːrd]
		v. to protect or keep safe from danger
		n. a person who protects others
		   guard a border → Many soldiers are **guarding** the border.
		   security guard → Matt works as a security **guard** at a bank.

11 independence
[indipéndəns]

n. the state of being free   syn freedom
gain one's independence
→ Korea gained its **independence** from Japan in 1945.

12 invade
[invéid]
n. invasion

v. to enter another land as an enemy   syn attack
invade a country
→ The enemy army **invaded** the country.

13 kill
[kil]

v. to make a person or other living thing die
kill a person
→ Influenza **kills** thousands of people every year.

14 mission
[míʃən]

n. an important task or duty   syn job
complete a mission
→ You must complete the **mission** in three days.

15 obstacle
[ábstəkl]

n. a difficulty that stops a person from doing something   syn problem
major obstacle
→ The cost is the major **obstacle** to the project.

16 risk
[risk]

n. a chance of injury, death, or danger
take a risk
→ She is taking a big **risk** by climbing the mountain.

17 shoot
[ʃuːt]
shoot - shot - shot

v. to fire a gun or other weapon
shoot at
→ The hunter **shot** at a rabbit next to a tree.

18 soldier
[sóuldʒər]

n. a person who fights in an army
serve as a soldier
→ He served as a **soldier** in the Korean War.

19 victory
[víktəri]

n. success in war, a game, etc.   syn win   ant loss
record a victory
→ The team recorded ten **victories** this year.

20 violent
[váiələnt]
n. violence

adj. using force to hurt, kill, or damage   ant peaceful
violent movie
→ Children should not watch **violent** movies.

A **Match the words with their definitions.**

1. soldier •   • a. to order others

2. damage •   • b. a person who fights in an army

3. shoot •   • c. to make a person or other living thing die

4. kill •   • d. a chance of injury, death, or danger

5. empire •   • e. to cause harm to someone or something

6. risk •   • f. to fire a gun or other weapon

7. command •   • g. a series of military, social, or political actions

8. campaign •   • h. a group of nations ruled by an emperor

B **Circle the two words in each group that are opposites.**

1. a. command   b. build   c. destroy   d. shoot

2. a. victory   b. independence   c. risk   d. loss

3. a. capture   b. attack   c. aim   d. defend

4. a. peaceful   b. empire   c. violent   d. campaign

C **Circle the words that best fit the sentences.**

1. There are too many obstacles | missions in the road.

2. The police invaded | captured the spy and took him to jail.

3. The soldiers are aiming | killing their guns at the enemy.

4. America gained its risk | independence from England in 1776.

5. She is going on a secret mission | guard into enemy land.

6. Some people are victory | violent and like to hurt others.

D Choose the correct words to complete the sentences.

1. The _____ at the front gate checked our IDs.

  a. guard   b. victory   c. empire   d. risk

2. The general wants to _____ the nearby country.

  a. shoot   b. kill   c. invade   d. capture

3. The bomb exploded and _____ the entire building.

  a. captured   b. destroyed   c. commanded   d. guarded

4. The hunter shot the deer with an _____.

  a. arrow   b. obstacle   c. independence   d. aim

5. He joined the army to become a _____.

  a. damage   b. mission   c. victory   d. soldier

E Read the passage. Then, fill in the blanks.

 Most countries around the world have armies. There are **soldiers** in their armies. Some armies are large while others are small. The **mission** of many armies is to **guard** and protect their countries. But some countries use their armies differently. Their armies **invade** other lands.

When this happens, a military **campaign** begins. The **soldiers** use their weapons. They **aim** at and **shoot** other people. They **kill** other **soldiers** and even regular people. They frequently **destroy** buildings and people's homes. Sometimes they **capture soldiers** and other people. These armies behave in a very **violent** manner. If the army wins, then the country's leaders declare **victory**. Of course, the people in the losing country want **independence**. So they often begin **campaigns** to win back their freedom.

1. Most armies have a _____ to guard their countries.

2. Some armies begin military _____ in other lands.

3. Invading armies may _____ buildings and homes.

4. People in losing countries begin campaigns to get their _____.

A Choose and write the correct words for the definitions.

| background | conductor | community | publish |
| textbook | shoot | command | review |

1. a book used in a classroom ➡ _____

2. the rear part of a scene, painting, etc. ➡ _____

3. a group of people who live in the same area ➡ _____

4. to order others ➡ _____

5. someone who directs the musicians in an orchestra ➡ _____

6. to go over something again ➡ _____

7. to fire a gun or other weapon ➡ _____

8. to print a book, newspaper, magazine, etc. ➡ _____

B Circle the words that are the most similar to the underlined words.

1. The teacher <u>encourages</u> the students to try hard.
   a. disagrees   b. admires   c. marries   d. inspires

2. Please try to <u>concentrate</u> while you are studying.
   a. compose   b. manage   c. focus   d. invent

3. The <u>purpose</u> of exercise is to get in good shape.
   a. empire   b. aim   c. obstacle   d. risk

4. The doctor said the boy's temperature was <u>normal</u>.
   a. average   b. total   c. clever   d. excellent

5. Helen likes to <u>imagine</u> that she is a pilot.
   a. pretend   b. cancel   c. exhibit   d. decorate

C Choose the correct forms of the words to complete the sentences.

1. It is a mystery | mysterious why it has not rained for months.

2. She thought of a good solve | solution to improve her grades.

3. The emperor | empire covers land all over the continent.

4. You need to behave | behavior better when you are at home.

5. He is trying to compose | composer a new song for the play.

D Complete the sentences with the words in the box.

1. It is rude to _____ people talking to you.

2. Sheila sings in the _____ every weekend.

3. The _____ is trying to fix the broken equipment.

4. Their _____ in the game made them the champions.

5. Tom created a _____ to help others in need.

> victory
>
> choir
>
> system
>
> ignore
>
> engineer

E Write the correct phrases in the blanks.

disagree with   organize a meeting   election campaign

writing a script   NASA astronaut   become a teenager

1. The _____ hopes to visit the moon.

2. I _____ you about the problem we have.

3. There are many ads on TV during an _____.

4. Steve is _____ for a new action movie.

5. Lewis will _____ on his next birthday.

6. Carl will _____ for the volunteers.

F Circle the mistakes. Then, write the correct sentences.

1. Try to concentration on the video you are watching.

➡ _____

2. Samantha and Tom will marriage each other next month.

➡ _____

3. Let's have a celebrate this coming weekend.

➡ _____

4. Aliens invasion the Earth in that story.

➡ _____

5. He manager a small grocery store in the town.

➡ _____

G Complete the crossword puzzle.

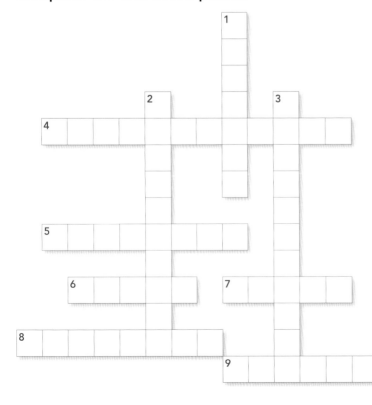

Across

4. relating to work that needs special training or skill

5. to study something carefully

6. clear, lively, or bright

7. to state why one is for or against something

8. a group of people watching a movie, game, etc.

9. to try to hurt or kill someone

Down

1. an important task or duty

2. the hard work and effort a person spends

3. very smart

H **Read the passage. Then, answer the questions below.**

Jim's Problem

Jim's parents have a problem. Jim is **intelligent** and is a **genius**. He gets **excellent** grades and never **cheats**. He always **behaves** well and is **generous**, too. He **composes** his own music. He wants to become an **astronaut** or **author** one day.

The problem is that he loves **violent** video games. He spends hours going on **missions** with his friends. They **shoot** and **kill** enemy **soldiers** and **destroy** land. His parents think the games are **realistic**, so they are **probably** not good for Jim.

Jim's parents want to change his **hobby**. So they register Jim for a **choir**. At first, he dislikes it. But he **pretends** to be a famous performer while singing. Jim **focuses** hard and becomes an **excellent** singer. He even sings solo during a **performance**. He loves his new **hobby**. And he stops playing **violent** video games.

1. What is the passage mainly about?

    a. what Jim and his parents like

    b. where Jim spends his time

    c. why Jim likes video games

    d. how Jim gets a new hobby

2. What does Jim want to be in the future?

    a. a video game designer   b. an astronaut

    c. a composer   d. a singer

3. Which is NOT true about Jim?

    a. He is intelligent.   b. He always behaves well.

    c. He gets poor grades.   d. He is generous.

4. What do Jim's parents think of video games?

    ➡ _____

5. Why do Jim's parents register Jim for a choir?

    ➡ _____

1 artificial
[ɑ̀ːrtifíʃəl]

adj. made by humans *ant* natural
artificial flower
→ She decorates her home with **artificial** flowers.

2 century
[séntʃəri]

n. a period lasting 100 years
twentieth century
→ The computer is the greatest invention of the **twentieth** century.

3 clearly
[klíərli]

adv. in a way that is easy to see or understand
explain clearly
→ Please explain your opinion **clearly**.

4 electric
[iléktrik]
n. electricity

adj. relating to or made by electricity
electric guitar
→ The musician plays the **electric** guitar very well.

5 extreme
[ikstríːm]

adj. great in degree
extreme poverty
→ Some Africans live in **extreme** poverty.

6 forecast
[fɔ́ːrkæ̀st]
forecast - forecast - forecast

n. a statement about what may happen *syn* guess
v. to make a statement about what may happen
weather forecast → The weather **forecast** calls for sunny skies.
forecast rain → The weatherman **forecasts** rain for tonight.

7 imagine
[imǽdʒin]
n. imagination

v. to form a picture of something in one's mind
imagine how
→ Can you **imagine** how it will look?

8 increase
[inkríːs]

v. to make bigger or larger in size, amount, etc. *ant* decrease
increase a price
→ The company has **increased** the price by 10%.

9 incredible
[inkrédəbl]
adv. incredibly

adj. amazing or hard to believe *syn* impressive
incredible speed
→ The plane flies at **incredible** speeds.

10 laboratory
[lǽbrətɔ̀ːri]

n. a room where people do experiments
science laboratory
→ The doctor is working in a science **laboratory**.

11 microwave
[máikrəwèiv]

n. an oven that cooks food quickly
v. to cook food in a microwave oven
    in a microwave → Heat the pizza in the **microwave**.
    microwave dinner → He **microwaves** dinner every night.

12 modern
[mádərn]

adj. relating to the present time   (ant) ancient
    modern art
    → I am interested in **modern** art.

13 operation
[àpəréiʃən]

n. the act of using or doing something; a medical procedure
    in operation → The machine has been in **operation** for ten years.
    knee operation → I had a knee **operation** last year.

14 satellite
[sǽtəlàit]

n. something that moves around another thing
    artificial satellite
    → There are many artificial **satellites** moving around the Earth.

15 scientific
[sàiəntífik]
n. science

adj. relating to science
    scientific study
    → The **scientific** study showed the dangers of pollution.

16 spaceship
[spéisʃìp]

n. a vehicle that can travel in space   (syn) spacecraft
    fly a spaceship
    → He will fly a **spaceship** to the moon.

17 telescope
[téliskòup]

n. an object used to make distant objects look bigger
    use a telescope
    → She used a **telescope** to look at Mars.

18 transport
[trænspɔ́ːrt]
n. transportation

v. to move people or things from one place to another   (syn) carry
    transport a passenger
    → Planes can **transport** passengers far distances.

19 vehicle
[víːhikl]

n. anything that can carry people or things
    motor vehicle
    → Many motor **vehicles** are on the roads.

20 vision
[víʒən]

n. the ability to see with the eyes   (syn) sight
    poor vision
    → She has poor **vision** and needs glasses.

Unit 11 Exercise

A **Circle the words that fit the definitions.**

1. to form a picture of something in one's mind

   a. imagine   b. forecast   c. transport   d. increase

2. relating to the present time

   a. scientific   b. artificial   c. extreme   d. modern

3. an object used to make distant objects look bigger

   a. laboratory   b. satellite   c. telescope   d. spaceship

4. the act of using or doing something

   a. century   b. vehicle   c. vision   d. operation

5. an oven that cooks food quickly

   a. satellite   b. microwave   c. forecast   d. laboratory

B **Write S for synonym or A for antonym next to each pair of words.**

1. _____ transport – carry   2. _____ forecast – guess

3. _____ modern – ancient   4. _____ incredible – impressive

5. _____ artificial – natural   6. _____ increase – decrease

C **Circle the words that best fit the sentences.**

1. Isaac Newton lived several laboratories | centuries ago.

2. The teacher told the students about the scientific | vehicle method.

3. Cell phones work thanks to satellites | forecasts in space.

4. We can see artificial | clearly from the top of the mountain.

5. I would love to take a spaceship | vision to the moon.

6. Clara was in modern | extreme pain after she broke her leg.

D **Choose the correct words to complete the sentences.**

1. He conducts many experiments in his _____.
   a. microwave   b. century   c. laboratory   d. telescope

2. I improved my _____ by wearing glasses.
   a. operation   b. vision   c. vehicle   d. spaceship

3. Her personal _____ is a small car.
   a. satellite   b. forecast   c. century   d. vehicle

4. The _____ light changed the way people lived.
   a. artificial   b. extreme   c. electric   d. modern

5. The ambulance will _____ the patient to the hospital.
   a. transport   b. imagine   c. increase   d. forecast

E **Read the passage. Then, write T for true or F for false.**

The twentieth **century** was **incredible**. People made all sorts of advances, so they created the **modern** world. For instance, one man invented the **microwave** oven in a **laboratory**. Thanks to him, millions of people use this **electric** oven to cook food. People developed all kinds of **vehicles**, too. They made cars, trucks, planes, and even **spaceships**. They **transport** people all around the Earth.

People made developments in space, too. Today, thousands of **satellites** move around the Earth. They let people use smartphones almost anywhere on the Earth. People can speak into their phones, and the listeners can hear them **clearly**. **Satellites** help with weather **forecasts**, too. So people can easily predict the weather now. These **scientific** developments have made the **modern** world a great time to be alive.

1. A man invented the microwave oven at his home. _____

2. People developed spaceships in the twentieth century. _____

3. Smartphones work thanks to electric lines. _____

4. People use satellites to make weather forecasts. _____

1	**accident** [ǽksidənt]	*n.* something often unpleasant that happens unexpectedly car accident → Nobody was hurt in the car **accident**.	
2	**amount** [əmáunt]	*n.* the sum of two or more numbers or amounts (syn) total final amount → What is the final **amount** I owe you?	
3	**arrest** [ərést]	*v.* to catch and hold a person for a certain crime (syn) capture arrest a thief → The police **arrested** the thief last night.	
4	**bad** [bæd] *adv.* badly	*adj.* not good (syn) poor (ant) excellent bad news → I have some **bad** news for you.	
5	**bite** [bait] bite - bit - bitten	*v.* to cut or tear with the teeth bite one's nails → When she feels nervous, she **bites** her nails.	
6	**bullet** [búlit]	*n.* a small ball fired from a gun shoot a bullet → This gun can shoot **bullets** quickly.	
7	**careless** [kéərləs]	*adj.* not exact or paying attention to what one does (ant) careful careless driver → Steve is a **careless** driver at times.	
8	**disabled** [diséibld]	*adj.* unable to use a part of the body properly disabled man → The **disabled** man cannot move his legs.	
9	**earthquake** [ə́ːrθkwèik]	*n.* a sudden shaking of the ground powerful earthquake → The powerful **earthquake** caused lots of damage.	
10	**emergency** [imə́ːrdʒənsi]	*n.* a sudden problem that must be solved at once medical emergency → I have a medical **emergency** and need a doctor.	

Unit 12

11 **hit**
[hit]
hit - hit - hit

v. to touch with force, often causing damage or injury; to strike
hit a bridge → The car **hit** the bridge at a fast speed.
hit a target → He **hit** the target with the weapon.

12 **mess**
[mes]
adj. messy

n. a dirty or untidy condition
make a mess
→ Do not make a **mess** on the floor.

13 **panic**
[pǽnik]

n. a sudden, strong feeling of anxiety or fear
in a panic
→ Everyone was in a **panic** during the fight.

14 **paralyze**
[pǽrəlàiz]

v. to make someone or something unable to move
paralyze an animal
→ The snake's venom can **paralyze** big animals.

15 **prison**
[prízən]

n. a building people who break the law are kept in   (syn) jail
go to prison
→ The man had to go to **prison** for five years.

16 **scare**
[skeər]
adj. scary

v. to make someone afraid   (syn) frighten
scare someone to death
→ The snake **scared** me to death.

17 **scream**
[skriːm]

v. to cry loudly, often in fear   (syn) yell
scream loudly
→ They **screamed** loudly while watching the scary movie.

18 **tragedy**
[trǽdʒədi]

n. a sad or unfortunate event
huge tragedy
→ It was a huge **tragedy** when the plane crashed.

19 **unbelievable**
[ʌnbilíːvəbl]

adj. difficult to believe and probably not true   (syn) impossible
unbelievable story
→ Ann told an **unbelievable** story about her dog.

20 **worse**
[wɜːrs]

adj. of poorer quality than something else   (ant) better
get worse
→ Jay got **worse**, so he went to see a doctor.

A   Match the words with their definitions.

1. bite •   • a. to cut or tear with the teeth

2. prison •   • b. a small ball fired from a gun

3. worse •   • c. to strike

4. paralyze •   • d. a building people who break the law are kept in

5. tragedy •   • e. a sudden shaking of the ground

6. hit •   • f. to make someone or something unable to move

7. earthquake •   • g. a sad or unfortunate event

8. bullet •   • h. of poorer quality than something else

B   Circle the two words in each group that have the same meaning.

1. a. scare   b. bite   c. frighten   d. arrest

2. a. total   b. mess   c. tragedy   d. amount

3. a. hit   b. scream   c. yell   d. paralyze

4. a. unbelievable   b. poor   c. careless   d. bad

C   Circle the words that best fit the sentences.

1. They took the patient to the bullet | emergency room at the hospital.

2. Karen helped the unbelievable | disabled man across the street.

3. He had an accident | amount while riding his bike.

4. The police will arrest | bite the criminal.

5. Do not be so careless | worse when you are driving.

6. There was mass prison | panic when someone shouted, "Fire!"

D Choose the correct words to complete the sentences.

1. Your bedroom is such a big _____.
   a. emergency   b. bullet   c. amount   d. mess

2. It is _____ how well he plays the trumpet.
   a. bad   b. unbelievable   c. worse   d. disabled

3. The big dog sometimes _____ people.
   a. arrests   b. screams   c. bites   d. paralyzes

4. The _____ destroyed several buildings.
   a. earthquake   b. amount   c. prison   d. panic

5. The loud noise _____ everyone in the room.
   a. screamed   b. arrested   c. hit   d. scared

E Read the passage. Then, fill in the blanks.

 **Earthquakes** happen when the ground begins to shake. Most of them are not very powerful. But some of them can be very strong. These **earthquakes** can cause a huge **panic**. They may destroy buildings and injure lots of people. The **amount** of damage they cause can be **unbelievable**.

A **bad earthquake** can **scare** people. Lots of people **scream** while the ground is shaking. Injured people may have to go to the **emergency** room. Most people recover from their injuries. But some people become **disabled**. For example, they may be **paralyzed**. Even **worse**, other people die. In these cases, **bad earthquakes** can be real **tragedies**. It is important to be prepared for an **earthquake**. Then, you will know what to do. So you might not be hurt badly.

1. When the ground shakes, _____ can happen.

2. Earthquakes that destroy buildings can cause a huge _____.

3. Some people hurt in earthquakes become _____.

4. Preparation for earthquakes can prevent real _____.

1	**able**
	[éibl]
	n. ability
		adj. having talent or the ability to do something
		  be able to
		  → Jack is **able** to speak French and Spanish.	

2	**alive**
	[əláiv]
		adj. having life; full of energy (syn) living (ant) dead
		  stay alive → He stayed **alive** during the war.
		  feel alive → I feel **alive** when I play music.	

3	**cough**
	[kɔ(ː)f]
		v. to breathe out air while making a sharp noise
		n. a time when one breathes out air while making a sharp noise
		  cough loudly → Joe **coughed** loudly all night long.
		  have a cough → He had a **cough** but feels better now.	

4	**fat**
	[fæt]
		adj. being overweight (ant) thin
		  become fat
		  → If you eat too much junk food, you'll become **fat**.	

5	**freeze**
	[friːz]
	freeze - froze - frozen
		v. to change from a liquid into ice or a solid (ant) melt
		  freeze slowly
		  → Water **freezes** slowly in cold weather.	

6	**injury**
	[índʒəri]
	v. injure
		n. harm or damage a person suffers from (syn) wound
		  get an injury
		  → She got an **injury** while jogging.	

7	**miracle**
	[mírəkl]
		n. an event that happens due to a supernatural reason
		  expect a miracle
		  → He expects a **miracle** to happen soon.	

8	**overweight**
	[òuvərwéit]
		adj. weighing more than normal
		  overweight luggage
		  → You can't take that **overweight** luggage on the plane.	

9	**pimple**
	[pímpl]
		n. a small, raised spot on the skin
		  pop a pimple
		  → Teens often pop **pimples** on their faces.	

10	**poison**
	[pɔ́izən]
	adj. poisonous
		n. a liquid that can cause harm or death if swallowed
		  contain poison
		  → That bottle contains **poison**, so do not drink it.	

11 proper
[prάpər]
adv. properly

adj. right, fitting, or appropriate　(syn) correct
proper manners
→ A gentleman should have **proper** manners

12 provide
[prəváid]

v. to give someone something that the person wants　(syn) supply
provide food
→ The school **provides** food for the students.

13 rapidly
[rǽpidli]
adj. rapid

adv. quickly　(ant) slowly
run rapidly
→ Cheetahs can run **rapidly**.

14 relieve
[rilí:v]

v. to ease or free from pain, worry, etc.
relieve one's pain
→ This medicine will **relieve** your pain.

15 sneeze
[sni:z]

v. to send out air suddenly from the mouth and the nose
make someone sneeze
→ Pepper makes people **sneeze** a lot.

16 soap
[soup]

n. something used to clean or wash with
soap and water
→ Wash your hands with **soap** and water.

17 sunlight
[sΛnlàit]

n. the light of the sun　(syn) sunshine
in the sunlight
→ They are relaxing in the **sunlight** at the pool.

18 tissue
[tíʃu:]

n. a group of cells in an animal or a plant
nerve tissue
→ She has a problem with her nerve **tissue**.

19 wound
[wu:nd]
adj. wounded

n. an injury, often involving a cut in the skin
heal a wound
→ The doctor will heal John's **wound**.

20 youth
[ju:θ]

n. the period of life involving one's childhood; the condition of being young
(ant) adult
waste one's youth → He wasted his **youth** by not studying hard.
in one's youth → She is fifteen and still in her **youth**.

A **Circle the words that fit the definitions.**

1. a liquid that can cause harm or death if swallowed

   a. soap   b. poison   c. cough   d. pimple

2. an injury, often involving a cut in the skin

   a. wound   b. pimple   c. sunlight   d. youth

3. to send out air suddenly from the mouth and the nose

   a. provide   b. relieve   c. sneeze   d. freeze

4. an event that happens due to a supernatural reason

   a. youth   b. injury   c. tissue   d. miracle

5. having talent or the ability to do something

   a. overweight   b. able   c. proper   d. alive

B **Choose and write the correct words for the blanks.**

alive	sunlight	youth	freeze	injury	provide

1. adult   ≠ _____   2. supply   = _____

3. wound   = _____   4. dead   ≠ _____

5. sunshine = _____   6. melt   ≠ _____

C **Circle the words that best fit the sentences.**

1. Put your hand over your mouth when you cough | provide .

2. The scientist is looking at the youth | tissue with a microscope.

3. Please wash your hands well with soap | miracle and water.

4. You should always wear proper | overweight clothes to work.

5. The cat is able | fat because it eats too much.

6. The car moved alive | rapidly down the highway.

D **Choose the correct words to complete the sentences.**

1. Teenagers often get _____ on their faces.
   a. miracles   b. coughs   c. pimples   d. tissues

2. You will become _____ if you eat too much candy.
   a. proper   b. overweight   c. able   d. alive

3. The medicine helped _____ her pain.
   a. relieve   b. freeze   c. provide   d. sneeze

4. It is important to spend some time in the _____ each day.
   a. sunlight   b. wound   c. tissue   d. injury

5. During his _____, he learned to play the violin.
   a. poison   b. soap   c. miracle   d. youth

E **Read the passage. Then, write T for true or F for false.**

Nowadays, many people are unhealthy in their **youth**. Some of them are very **fat**. They become **overweight** by eating too much junk food. They have **pimples** from eating junk food, too. They also do not get enough **sunlight**. They prefer to stay indoors and rarely go outside. They get sick often, so they frequently **cough** and **sneeze**. Some of them get **injuries** easily.

However, people are **able** to improve their health in their **youth**. There are many ways to do this. First, they can take good care of themselves. They can wash their hands with **soap** frequently. They can eat **proper** food that is nutritious. They can go outside and exercise. By doing these activities, young people can have happy and healthy lives.

1. Some young people have pimples because they are fat. _____

2. Many young people stay indoors so do not get enough sunlight. _____

3. People can be healthy by eating proper junk food. _____

4. By doing outside activities, young people can be healthy. _____

1	**actual** [ǽktʃuəl] *adv.* actually	*adj.* real or existing now actual truth → Please tell me the **actual** truth.

2	**appear** [əpíər] *n.* appearance	*v.* to become visible; to look like (syn) seem (ant) disappear suddenly appear → A UFO suddenly **appeared** in the sky. appear happy → The students all **appear** happy.

3	**brief** [briːf]	*adj.* lasting a short time (syn) quick (ant) long brief rainstorm → There was a **brief** rainstorm last night.

4	**deeply** [díːpli]	*adv.* very much deeply shocked → She was **deeply** shocked by the news.

5	**differ** [dífər] *n.* difference	*v.* to be unlike someone or something differ in → They are twins but **differ** in appearance.

6	**ease** [iːz]	*v.* to reduce the effects of ease one's pain → The medicine quickly **eased** her pain.

7	**elder** [éldər]	*adj.* of greater age (syn) older (ant) younger elder brother → Carol has two **elder** brothers.

8	**equal** [íːkwəl]	*adj.* the same as (syn) alike (ant) different equal rights → Women demanded **equal** rights in the past.

9	**hug** [hʌg]	*v.* to hold a person in one's arms *n.* the act of holding a person in one's arms hug tightly → She **hugged** her baby tightly. give a hug → Amy gave her mother a big **hug**.

10	**nickname** [níknèim]	*n.* an informal name for a person or thing have a nickname → Dave has a **nickname** his friends gave him.

11 normal
[nɔ́ːrməl]

adj. being common or usual (syn) ordinary
normal behavior
→ His **normal** behavior at school is good.

12 opposite
[ɑ́pəzit]

adj. very different from something else
opposite directions
→ The two men drove in **opposite** directions.

13 pair
[peər]

n. two identical things; something with two parts put together
pair of gloves → There is a **pair** of gloves on the table.
pair of scissors → Please lend me a **pair** of scissors.

14 patient
[péiʃənt]

adj. able to wait without complaint
n. a person getting medical treatment
patient person → Susan is a very **patient** person nowadays.
cure a patient → The doctor is busy curing **patients**.

15 personal
[pə́rsənəl]
n. personality

adj. relating to a certain person (syn) private
personal subject
→ I do not like to talk about **personal** subjects with some people.

16 private
[práivət]
n. privacy

adj. belonging to a certain person
private property
→ They cannot come onto this **private** property.

17 realize
[rí(ː)əlàiz]

v. to understand something clearly
realize the truth
→ He suddenly **realized** the truth and got upset.

18 respect
[rispékt]

n. a very good opinion of someone
v. to have a very good opinion of someone (syn) admire
great respect → They showed great **respect** to the king.
respect someone → I really **respect** my teacher.

19 similar
[símələr]
n. similarity

adj. almost the same (syn) alike (ant) different
similar story
→ All the children told **similar** stories.

20 terrific
[tərífik]

adj. very good or wonderful (syn) excellent (ant) terrible
terrific view
→ You can see a **terrific** view at the top of the mountain.

A   **Circle the correct definitions for the given words.**

1. respect
    a. an informal name for a person or thing   b. a very good opinion of someone
    c. two identical things   d. a person getting medical treatment

2. ease
    a. to understand something clearly   b. to hold a person in one's arms
    c. to reduce the effects of   d. to become visible

3. patient
    a. able to wait without complaint   b. very good or wonderful
    c. lasting a short time   d. almost the same

4. normal
    a. of greater age   b. belonging to a certain person
    c. real or existing now   d. being common or usual

B   **Circle the two words in each group that are opposites.**

1. a. different   b. private   c. similar   d. patient

2. a. equal   b. brief   c. actual   d. long

3. a. differ   b. disappear   c. appear   d. respect

4. a. terrible   b. personal   c. opposite   d. terrific

C   **Circle the words that best fit the sentences.**

1. Karen has an elder | opposite brother.

2. I have a similar | personal favor to ask of you.

3. Please give me a nickname | pair of scissors.

4. We were having a private | patient conversation.

5. Both of them weigh an actual | equal amount.

6. He always hugs | differs his grandparents when he sees them.

D **Choose the correct words to complete the sentences.**

1. He told us the _____ events that happened to him.
   a. actual   b. patient   c. deeply   d. elder

2. They are standing on _____ sides of the river.
   a. opposite   b. normal   c. terrific   d. private

3. An alligator and a crocodile _____ in many ways.
   a. ease   b. appear   c. differ   d. respect

4. Tom would not tell us his _____.
   a. respect   b. nickname   c. pair   d. hug

5. I suddenly _____ that I had given the wrong answer.
   a. appeared   b. easied   c. hugged   d. realized

E **Read the passage. Then, fill in the blanks.**

It is important to act properly toward other people. So the following is a **brief** lesson on good manners.

A person should always show **respect** to people who are **elder**. This is **normal** behavior for people with good manners. A person with good manners should also be **patient**. The person should understand that people **differ** from one another. Some of them have similar personalities. But many of them have **opposite** personalities. Yet they can still get along easily.

To be polite, a person should not ask **personal** questions. Many people are **private** individuals. They do not like to talk about **personal** topics. They might not even like to talk about their own **nicknames**. So show some **respect** to others, and you can have **terrific** relationships with them.

1. People need to show _____ to those older than them.

2. People may have both similar and _____ personalities.

3. It is not polite to ask people _____ questions.

4. Show respect to others to have _____ relationships with them.

1	**avenue** [ǽvənjùː]	*n.* a wide street (syn) road long avenue → There is a long **avenue** going through the city.
2	**construction** [kənstrʌ́kʃən] *v.* construct	*n.* the act of building a house, bridge, etc. under construction → The apartment building is under **construction** now.
3	**describe** [diskráib]	*v.* to tell or write about something describe a person → Please **describe** the person you saw.
4	**downstairs** [daunstéərz]	*adv.* to a lower floor (ant) upstairs go downstairs → Go **downstairs** to get to the restaurant.
5	**drawer** [drɔːr]	*n.* a sliding part of a piece of furniture that holds things open a drawer → Open the **drawer** and find a T-shirt.
6	**exit** [égzit]	*n.* a door leading out of a room or building *v.* to leave a room or building (ant) enter fire exit → Use the fire **exit** during an emergency. exit a building → Please **exit** the building quickly.
7	**front** [frʌnt]	*n.* the part of something facing forward (ant) back in front of → He is standing in **front** of the students.
8	**furniture** [fɜ́ːrnitʃər]	*n.* items like chairs, beds, etc. used in houses and offices wood furniture → I bought some wood **furniture** at the store.
9	**handkerchief** [hǽŋkərtʃi(ː)f]	*n.* a small cloth used to wipe parts of a person's face pocket handkerchief → John always carries a pocket **handkerchief**.
10	**heritage** [héritidʒ]	*n.* something handed down from the past (syn) tradition national heritage → We should all preserve our national **heritage**.

11	**item** [áitəm]	*n.* a separate thing personal item → You can take some personal **items** on the trip.
12	**niece** [niːs]	*n.* a daughter of one's brother or sister young niece → I have a young **niece** who is five.
13	**property** [prápərti]	*n.* something a person owns public property → The parks in the city are public **property**.
14	**repair** [ripéər]	*v.* to fix something that is broken *ant* break repair a car → The mechanic can **repair** cars very well.
15	**spare** [speər]	*adj.* kept to be used later *syn* extra spare tire → She keeps a **spare** tire in her car's trunk.
16	**supper** [sʌ́pər]	*n.* an evening meal *syn* dinner eat supper → What time do you usually eat **supper**?
17	**swing** [swiŋ] swing - swung - swung	*v.* to move back and forth from a fixed point swing slowly → The rope is **swinging** slowly back and forth.
18	**usual** [júːʒuəl] *adv.* usually	*adj.* common or everyday *syn* normal *ant* unusual as usual → As **usual**, class started at 9:00 AM.
19	**warm** [wɔːrm] *n.* warmth	*adj.* having a small amount of heat *ant* cool warm weather → Korea gets **warm** weather in spring.
20	**within** [wiðín]	*prep.* in or inside *ant* outside within a room → The missing keys are somewhere **within** the room.

A **Match the words with their definitions.**

1. usual •   • a. the act of building a house, bridge, etc.

2. swing •   • b. to move back and forth from a fixed point

3. describe •   • c. something handed down from the past

4. niece •   • d. something a person owns

5. heritage •   • e. common or everyday

6. construction •   • f. a separate thing

7. property •   • g. a daughter of one's brother or sister

8. item •   • h. to tell or write about something

B **Choose and write the correct words for the blanks.**

spare	heritage	within	warm	avenue	exit

1. road   = _____

2. outside ≠ _____

3. tradition = _____

4. enter   ≠ _____

5. cool   ≠ _____

6. extra   = _____

C **Circle the words that best fit the sentences.**

1. You can find some pencils in the drawer | handkerchief .

2. Mr. Peters will repair | exit the broken bicycle.

3. We usually eat heritage | supper around seven in the evening.

4. Jane is standing at the front | construction of the line.

5. I found a strange avenue | item in the box.

6. Go within | downstairs to get to the basement.

D **Choose the correct words to complete the sentences.**

1. He carries a _____ to wipe his nose with.

   a. handkerchief   b. front   c. construction   d. supper

2. The shop is located on Fifth _____ in the city.

   a. Item   b. Avenue   c. Drawer   d. Property

3. Please _____ the store before it closes in ten minutes.

   a. describe   b. repair   c. swing   d. exit

4. I do not have any _____ money to lend you.

   a. usual   b. warm   c. spare   d. within

5. The store sells _____ like sofas and beds.

   a. furniture   b. front   c. niece   d. heritage

E **Read the passage. Then, write T for true or F for false.**

 One day, Susan's father gives his family some news. He purchased a **property** in the countryside. He is going to build a new house on it. The **construction** of the house takes more than one year. Then, Susan and her family move into the house.
Susan's father **describes** the house. It is much bigger than their previous home. There are five bedrooms. They are for Susan, her parents, and her brother, and there are two **spare** ones. There is lots of room for all of their **furniture**, too. Susan's bedroom is on the second floor. She loves running **downstairs** when it is time to eat. There is a big tree in **front** of the **exit**. There is a tire hanging from the tree. Susan enjoys **swinging** back and forth on it.

1. Susan and her family have a property downtown.   _____

2. The construction of Susan's home takes less than one year.   _____

3. Susan's new house has two spare bedrooms.   _____

4. Susan has to go downstairs when it is time to eat.   _____

A Choose and write the correct words for the definitions.

bite	miracle	opposite	tragedy
describe	satellite	deeply	vehicle

1. to cut or tear with the teeth ➡ _____

2. something that moves around another thing ➡ _____

3. to tell or write about something ➡ _____

4. a sad or unfortunate event ➡ _____

5. an event that happens due to a supernatural reason ➡ _____

6. very much ➡ _____

7. anything that can carry people or things ➡ _____

8. very different from something else ➡ _____

B Circle the words that are the most similar to the underlined words.

1. It is rude to ask people about their <u>private</u> lives.
   a. patient   b. equal   c. personal   d. actual

2. The farmer can <u>supply</u> all the food that we need.
   a. provide   b. freeze   c. relieve   d. cough

3. There are some <u>extra</u> tools in the storage room.
   a. warm   b. spare   c. usual   d. normal

4. The man is in <u>jail</u> for stealing from a store.
   a. emergency   b. prison   c. panic   d. accident

5. The truck will <u>carry</u> food to the city.
   a. forecast   b. increase   c. imagine   d. transport

C Choose the correct forms of the words to complete the sentences.

1. The construct | construction project is almost finished.

2. It is incredibly | incredible how strong that man is.

3. Are you able | ability to give us some help tomorrow?

4. Her bedroom is a huge mess | messy .

5. The two boys look very similarity | similar to each other.

D Complete the sentences with the words in the box.

1. The Roman Empire ended many _____ ago.

2. Please cover your mouth when you _____.

3. I hope that we get some _____ weather soon.

4. Children like to _____ others on Halloween.

5. The _____ story is really amazing.

warm
actual
centuries
scare
cough

E Write the correct phrases in the blanks.

in a panic	appears happy	patient person
fire exit	knee operation	contains poison

1. Doug is a _____ and does not mind waiting.

2. Some people were _____ during the storm.

3. Every building must have a _____.

4. The bottle over there _____.

5. Suzie _____ with her science grade.

6. Linda's _____ was a complete success.

F **Circle the mistakes. Then, write the correct sentences.**

1. His wounded is healing very slowly.

   ➡ _____

2. Refrigerators are popular electricity appliances.

   ➡ _____

3. Her usually breakfast is bacon, eggs, and toast.

   ➡ _____

4. He made a badly mistake during the play.

   ➡ _____

5. Please explain how the two animals difference.

   ➡ _____

G **Complete the crossword puzzle.**

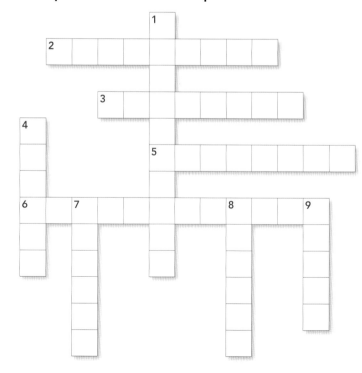

Across

2. an oven that cooks food quickly
3. the light of the sun
5. very good or wonderful
6. difficult to believe and probably not true

Down

1. to a lower floor
4. harm or damage a person suffers from
7. a small ball fired from a gun
8. a wide street
9. the same as

H **Read the passage. Then, answer the questions below.**

Emily and Kate

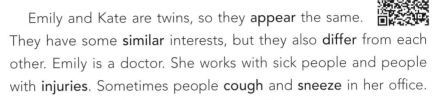

Emily and Kate are twins, so they **appear** the same. They have some **similar** interests, but they also **differ** from each other. Emily is a doctor. She works with sick people and people with **injuries**. Sometimes people **cough** and **sneeze** in her office. She gives them the **proper** medicine. She says they should get lots of **sunlight** and wash their hands with **soap**.

Kate works in a **scientific laboratory**. She is interested in **spaceships** and **satellites**. She is trying to create a new **vehicle**. It will **transport** people into space one day.

The twins have **opposite** personalities. Emily is **patient** and careful. She is also neat, so she cleans her room every day. But Kate is impatient and **careless**. So she often breaks her glasses. And she makes a **mess** in her room. However, they get along with each other.

1. What is the passage mainly about?

 a. the reasons twins are often alike

 b. similarities and differences in two sisters

 c. the jobs that Emily and Kate have

 d. the personalities of two twins

2. What do some people do in Emily's office?

 a. They get injured.　　　　　　　b. They wash their hands.

 c. They take medicine.　　　　　　d. They cough and sneeze.

3. What does Kate want to do?

 a. fly to the moon　　　　　　　　b. develop some medicine

 c. make a new spaceship　　　　　d. teach students

4. What does Emily tell her patients to do?

 ➡ _____

5. What is Emily's personality?

 ➡ _____

1 absorb
[əbsɔ́:rb]

v. to take in a liquid or gas

absorb water

→ A sponge can **absorb** a lot of water.

2 aloud
[əláud]

adv. in a voice that other people can hear   (syn) clearly   (ant) quietly

speak aloud

→ You should not speak **aloud** during the talk.

3 aware
[əwéər]

adj. having knowledge; paying close attention

aware of a fact → I am **aware** of that fact already.

aware of danger → They are **aware** of danger in the jungle.

4 beauty
[bjú:ti]
adj. beautiful

n. the quality of looking good to the eye

full of beauty

→ The painting he made is full of **beauty**.

5 bitter
[bítər]

adj. having an unpleasant taste   (ant) sweet

bitter taste

→ Some fruits have a **bitter** taste.

6 calm
[kɑ:m]

adj. not rough, windy, or excited   (syn) quiet

calm personality

→ Allen has a very **calm** personality.

7 clap
[klæp]

v. to hit one's hands to make noise

clap one's hands

→ He **clapped** his hands several times.

8 dirty
[dɔ́:rti]
n. dirt

adj. not clean   (ant) neat

dirty floor

→ Please sweep the **dirty** floor right now.

9 feather
[féðər]

n. the outer covering of a bird

tail feather

→ The tail **feathers** of a bird help it fly.

10 flow
[flou]

v. to move like a liquid

flow quickly

→ The water in the river is **flowing** quickly.

11 fur
[fɜːr]

n. the soft, thick, hairy covering of an animal
    fur coat
    → Some people wear **fur** coats in winter.

12 heat
[hiːt]

n. the state of having a lot of warmth
v. to make something hot   (ant) cool
    feel the heat → I felt the **heat** of the sun on my back.
    heat a home → Many people **heat** their homes with gas.

13 nod
[nɑd]

v. to move one's head forward to show agreement or understanding
    nod in agreement
    → Jake **nodded** his head in agreement.

14 pour
[pɔːr]

v. to make a liquid flow or fall from a container
    pour a drink
    → I **poured** a drink into a glass.

15 quality
[kwɑ́ləti]

n. how good or bad something is; high grade   (syn) excellence
    high quality → The products at the store are high **quality**.
    quality work → He did **quality** work on the house.

16 raw
[rɔː]

adj. not cooked   (syn) fresh
    raw fish
    → **Raw** fish is a popular food in Japan.

17 rub
[rʌb]

v. to move something back and forth over a surface
    rub one's hands
    → She **rubbed** her hands together to clean them.

18 smooth
[smuːð]

adj. flat and not rough   (syn) even
    smooth road
    → It is a **smooth** road with no holes in it.

19 squeeze
[skwiːz]

v. to press something firmly
    squeeze a lemon
    → I **squeezed** the lemon to get some juice.

20 unusual
[ʌnjúːʒuəl]

adj. different or not normal   (syn) strange   (ant) usual
    unusual weather
    → We are getting **unusual** weather this winter.

A   Circle the correct definitions for the given words.

1. clap
   a. to make something hot
   b. to take in a liquid or gas
   c. to move like a liquid
   d. to hit one's hands to make noise

2. quality
   a. the outer covering of a bird
   b. the soft, thick, hairy covering of an animal
   c. how good or bad something is
   d. the state of having a lot of warmth

3. bitter
   a. having an unpleasant taste
   b. paying close attention
   c. not clean
   d. not rough, windy, or excited

4. aware
   a. flat and not rough
   b. having knowledge
   c. different or not normal
   d. not cooked

B   Circle the two words in each group that have the same meaning.

1. a. strange   b. dirty   c. unusual   d. bitter

2. a. raw   b. rub   c. nod   d. fresh

3. a. absorb   b. calm   c. quiet   d. squeeze

4. a. aloud   b. even   c. aware   d. smooth

C   Circle the words that best fit the sentences.

1. I cannot believe you said that aware | aloud .

2. She nodded | poured her head to show she agreed.

3. Flow | Rub your hands together with lots of soap.

4. You can clap | squeeze the towel to get the water out.

5. Please heat | absorb the water so we can boil the eggs.

6. The peacock has some beautiful tail furs | feathers .

D Choose the correct words to complete the sentences.

1. The ground _____ all of the rain that fell.

    a. flowed   b. clapped   c. squeezed   d. absorbed

2. The bear's thick _____ keeps it warm in winter.

    a. quality   b. fur   c. heat   d. feather

3. The water in the river is _____ very fast.

    a. flowing   b. heating   c. rubbing   d. pouring

4. I cannot believe how _____ the room was.

    a. aware   b. raw   c. dirty   d. bitter

5. You must _____ the oil into the flour and mix them together.

    a. pour   b. rub   c. clap   d. nod

E Read the passage. Then, fill in the blanks.

Because of the **heat** of summer, people like to take trips to get away from hot places. Camping trips are a bit **unusual**, but some people enjoy taking them. They can see the **beauty** of the natural environment.

These people usually go to a forest. They like to find a **calm** and quiet place. Some campers stay beside water such as a river or stream. They want to see water **flowing** down the river or stream. They enjoy going fishing and then eating **raw** fish. Others prefer to stay away from water. They instead stay in a forest surrounded by trees. They are **aware** of the sights and smells of the forest. They can enjoy walking on **smooth** grass in their bare feet. There, they might find some bird **feathers**.

1. People may take trips due to the _____ of summer.

2. Some people want to see the _____ of the natural environment.

3. Campers often prefer a _____ and quiet place.

4. Some campers go fishing and eat _____ fish.

1 adapt
[ədǽpt]

v. to change something so it fits better

adapt to

→ It takes time to **adapt** to a foreign culture.

2 affect
[æfékt]

v. to have an effect on something   *syn* influence

affect greatly

→ The weather **affects** our lives greatly.

3 ancient
[éinʃənt]

adj. very old   *ant* modern

ancient history

→ Jane is reading a book about **ancient** history.

4 common
[kámən]

adj. usual or everyday   *syn* normal   *ant* rare

common knowledge

→ The name of the president is **common** knowledge.

5 conclusion
[kənklú:ʒən]
v. conclude

n. the end or a final part   *ant* start

sad conclusion

→ *Romeo and Juliet* has a sad **conclusion**.

6 debate
[dibéit]

v. to have a discussion
n. a discussion with opposite views

debate something → They are **debating** the new law.
hold a debate → They will hold a **debate** tonight.

7 detail
[díteil]

n. a small fact or item

in detail

→ Let's talk about the topic in **detail**.

8 discover
[diskʌ́vər]
n. discovery

v. to see, learn about, or find for the first time   *syn* notice

discover America

→ Columbus **discovered** America in 1492.

9 discuss
[diskʌ́s]
n. discussion

v. to talk about something, often in detail   *syn* debate

discuss a topic

→ They will **discuss** the topic tomorrow.

10 documentary
[dɑ̀kjuméntəri]

n. a TV program or movie based on facts

watch a documentary

→ They will watch a **documentary** about lions.

11 education
[èdʒukéiʃən]
v. educate

n. the act of teaching or learning
good education
→ Amy got a good **education** at her school.

12 expert
[ékspɜːrt]

n. a person with special skills or knowledge about something
expert on
→ John is an **expert** on computers.

13 figure
[fígjər]

n. a number
v. to work with numbers
low figure → The salesman's offer was a low **figure**.
figure out → Use a calculator to **figure** out the answer.

14 lecture
[léktʃər]

n. a talk to a group of people about a topic   (syn) class
give a lecture
→ The teacher gave a **lecture** on history.

15 principal
[prínsəpəl]

adj. first or more important   (syn) main
n. the head of a school
principal reason → What was the **principal** reason for the fire?
talk to a principal → Talk to the **principal** about your problem.

16 riddle
[rídl]

n. a puzzling question or problem
solve a riddle
→ Nobody can solve the **riddle**.

17 scholar
[skάlər]

n. a person who knows a lot about a certain subject
famous scholar
→ He became a famous **scholar** of history.

18 suppose
[səpóuz]

v. to think that something is true
suppose that
→ **Suppose** that it rains tomorrow.

19 survey
[sɜ́ːrvei]

n. the act of taking a general view of something
carry out a survey
→ We need to carry out a **survey**.

20 valuable
[vǽljuəbl]

adj. worth a lot of money; very useful or important   (ant) worthless
valuable ring → She is wearing a **valuable** gold ring.
valuable experience → Visiting the museum was a **valuable** experience.

A Circle the words that fit the definitions.

1. to change something so it fits better

a. discover   b. suppose   c. adapt   d. affect

2. very useful or important

a. valuable   b. common   c. ancient   d. principal

3. a person who knows a lot about a certain subject

a. survey   b. lecture   c. principal   d. scholar

4. a discussion with opposite views

a. expert   b. conclusion   c. debate   d. education

5. to work with numbers

a. affect   b. figure   c. discuss   d. suppose

B Write S for synonym or A for antonym next to each pair of words.

1. _____ conclusion – start

2. _____ common – rare

3. _____ affect – influence

4. _____ ancient – modern

5. _____ principal – main

6. _____ lecture – class

C Circle the words that best fit the sentences.

1. I suppose | adapt that she could be right.

2. Sharon is a well-known detail | expert on lions and tigers.

3. Nobody could solve the lecture | riddle he told.

4. Let's discuss | affect this problem right now.

5. The students love to watch documentaries | figures on animals.

6. Students go to school to get a good survey | education .

D **Choose the correct words to complete the sentences.**

1. We do not know all of the _____ about the new product.
   a. documentaries   b. details   c. experts   d. lectures

2. He took a _____ online and answered several questions.
   a. debate   b. survey   c. riddle   d. principal

3. The scientist hopes to _____ a cure for the disease.
   a. affect   b. adapt   c. suppose   d. discover

4. Humans lived different lives in _____ times.
   a. principal   b. valuable   c. ancient   d. common

5. At the _____ of the story, the couple gets married.
   a. conclusion   b. figure   c. scholar   d. education

E **Read the passage. Then, write T for true or F for false.**

At Central High School, every student gets a great **education**. All of the teachers at the school are **scholars**. So they are **experts** in their fields because they know many things about their subjects. When the teachers give **lectures** to the students, they teach the students **valuable** information.

For example, in Mr. Patterson's class, the students study **ancient** history. In his class, they **discover** lots of interesting facts about the past. Mr. Patterson even makes up **riddles** about history sometimes. The students have fun trying to solve them. In some classes, he does not give **lectures** to the students. Instead, he lets them **debate** the past. So the students **discuss** historical events in **detail**. Thanks to Mr. Patterson, all of the students learn a lot about history.

1. The students at Central High School are all scholars.   _____

2. The teachers provide information when they give lectures.   _____

3. Students make up riddles in Mr. Patterson's history class.   _____

4. The students in history class sometimes debate the past.   _____

1 apply
[əplái]

v. to use; formally to request something such as a job
apply one's learning → **Apply** your learning to this lesson.
apply for → She **applied** for a job at MRT, Inc.

2 appoint
[əpɔ́int]
n. appointment

v. to name a person to a position   syn hire
appoint a president
→ They need to **appoint** a new president.

3 article
[á:rtikl]

n. a piece of writing in a newspaper or magazine
newspaper article
→ I'm reading an interesting newspaper **article**.

4 cash
[kæʃ]

n. coins or bills
in cash
→ Do you want to pay in **cash** or by credit card?

5 congratulate
[kəngrǽtʃəlèit]
n. congratulation

v. to express happiness to a person for doing something
congratulate for
→ We **congratulated** her for winning the prize.

6 customer
[kʌ́stəmər]

n. a person who buys goods or services   syn shopper
help a customer
→ The salesman is busy helping the **customer**.

7 department
[dipá:rtmənt]

n. a section in a school, business, etc.
Sales Department
→ John works in the Sales **Department**.

8 disadvantage
[dìsədvǽntidʒ]

n. the state of being in a bad situation or condition   ant advantage
at a disadvantage
→ Our team is at a **disadvantage** now.

9 goods
[gudz]

n. things produced for sale   syn products
sell goods
→ The store sells many kinds of sporting **goods**.

10 interview
[íntərvjù:]

n. a meeting in which someone is asked questions
v. to ask questions at a meeting
job interview → I have a job **interview** today.
interview for a job → He **interviewed** for a job at TRT, Inc.

11 law
[lɔː]
n. lawyer

n. the rules that people must follow
break the law
→ You should not break the **law** by stealing.

12 practical
[prǽktikəl]

adj. realistic or being useful
practical lesson
→ Mr. Jones always teaches **practical** lessons.

13 presentation
[prìːzəntéiʃən]

n. the act of speaking about something
give a presentation
→ Tim will give a **presentation** to his class.

14 regular
[régjələr]
adv. regularly

adj. usual or common   (syn) normal
regular activity
→ Cycling is one of my **regular** activities.

15 reply
[riplái]

v. to answer a question   (syn) respond   (ant) ask
n. an answer to a question
reply to → You should **reply** to your parents' questions.
make no reply → Angie made no **reply** to the letter.

16 separate
[sépəreit][séprət]

v. to keep apart   (syn) divide   (ant) unite
adj. unconnected or different
separate into → Please **separate** into small groups.
separate lives → The two brothers live **separate** lives.

17 serve
[sɜːrv]
n. service

v. to work for or provide help to
serve someone
→ She **served** her boss well for years.

18 supply
[səplái]

v. to provide something needed
supply food
→ The charity **supplies** food to poor people.

19 tax
[tæks]

n. money people must pay the government
pay tax
→ They pay their **taxes** once a year.

20 wealthy
[wélθi]

adj. having a lot of money   (syn) rich   (ant) poor
be wealthy
→ He is **wealthy** enough to buy a big house.

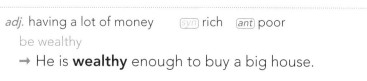

Unit 18 Exercise

A **Match the words with their definitions.**

1. serve •   • a. money people must pay the government

2. cash •   • b. to work for or provide help to

3. presentation •   • c. coins or bills

4. interview •   • d. a section in a school, business, etc.

5. tax •   • e. to ask questions at a meeting

6. supply •   • f. realistic or being useful

7. department •   • g. to provide something needed

8. practical •   • h. the act of speaking about something

B **Circle the two words in each group that are opposites.**

1. a. wealthy   b. poor   c. regular   d. practical

2. a. serve   b. interview   c. unite   d. separate

3. a. apply   b. ask   c. supply   d. reply

4. a. disadvantage   b. article   c. advantage   d. law

C **Circle the words that best fit the sentences.**

1. This online store has lots of customers | goods at low prices.

2. It is time for Janet's regular | wealthy checkup at the doctor.

3. John plans to reply | apply for a position at a big company.

4. You must follow the interview | law and not break it.

5. Some customers | articles asked the manager about refunds.

6. The president congratulated | supplied her after she won a gold medal.

D Choose the correct words to complete the sentences.

1. He wrote a long _____ about the economy for a magazine.

    a. article   b. cash   c. department   d. customer

2. The CEO _____ Harry the new vice president.

    a. separated   b. supplied   c. replied   d. appointed

3. Please name one _____ of taking the bus to school.

    a. presentation   b. law   c. disadvantage   d. tax

4. I sent April a letter, but she did not _____ to me.

    a. serve   b. reply   c. apply   d. interview

5. He started his own company and became a _____ man.

    a. practical   b. separate   c. regular   d. wealthy

E Read the passage. Then, fill in the blanks.

    Ms. Jenkins decides to open a store. First, she studies the **law**. She learns she must **apply** for a permit from the city. She finds a place for her store. Then, she **interviews** some workers. She **appoints** the best worker as the store manager.

    Finally, she is ready to open the store. On the first day, lots of **customers** come. They buy all kinds of **goods** at the store. She earns very much **cash** on the first day. Everyone **congratulates** her on the success of her store. However, she realizes that her store has one big **disadvantage**. It has no website. She decides to make an online store. Then, she can sell even more **goods**. Ms. Jenkins hopes she becomes **wealthy** by running her store.

1. Ms. Jenkins _____ for a permit from the city.

2. Ms. Jenkins _____ one of the workers as the manager.

3. Many _____ visit the store on the first day.

4. One _____ is that the store has no website.

1	**allow** [əláu] n. allowance	v. to let someone do something allow in → They do not **allow** the cat in the bathroom.
2	**chase** [tʃeis]	v. to run after to try to catch (syn) follow chase after → The police are **chasing** after the bank robber.
3	**compare** [kəmpéər]	v. to say how two things are similar and different compare grades → The students **compare** grades with one another.
4	**custom** [kʌ́stəm]	n. something a person regularly does; a tradition (syn) habit good custom → His family has many good **customs**. Christmas custom → Giving gifts is a Christmas **custom**.
5	**encourage** [inkʌ́ːridʒ] n. encouragement	v. to make a person braver or more confident (syn) inspire encourage someone → He **encourages** his students to do their best.
6	**exist** [igzíst]	v. to be or live still exist → The house is old but still **exists**.
7	**fact** [fækt]	n. something that is true or happened in the past (syn) truth in fact → In **fact**, Bill won the contest.
8	**generally** [dʒénərəli]	adv. usually (syn) commonly generally speaking → **Generally** speaking, I dislike driving.
9	**host** [houst]	n. a person who invites guests be a host → Kevin will be the **host** of the party.
10	**include** [inklúːd]	v. to contain something as a part include tax → The price doesn't **include** tax.

11 instruct
[instrʌ́kt]
n. instruction

v. to teach; to tell someone to do something   syn train
   instruct students → Ms. Wilson **instructs** students in math.
   instruct someone → The police **instructed** him to be quiet

12 list
[list]

n. a set of names, numbers, etc.
v. to write a set of names, numbers, etc.
   shopping list → What is on your shopping **list**?
   list one's chores → Karen **listed** her chores for the day.

13 nearly
[níərli]

adv. almost
   not nearly
   → This is not **nearly** enough money.

14 notice
[nóutis]

v. to become aware of   syn observe   ant ignore
n. an announcement that something will happen
   notice someone → I didn't **notice** her leaving.
   post a notice → We posted the **notice** on the board.

15 particular
[pərtíkjələr]

adj. relating to a single person, place, thing, etc.
   no particular reason
   → I stayed home for no **particular** reason.

16 safety
[séifti]
adj. safe

n. the state of being free from danger   ant risk
   lead to safety
   → The fireman led the people to **safety**.

17 since
[sins]

prep. between a past time and the present
   since last winter
   → The weather has changed a lot **since** last winter.

18 typical
[típikəl]

adj. usual   syn normal   ant unusual
   typical day
   → Her **typical** day starts early in the morning.

19 unlike
[ʌnláik]

prep. different or not equal
   unlike each other
   → The twins are really **unlike** each other.

20 weekly
[wí:kli]

adj. happening once every seven days
   weekly magazine
   → She buys the **weekly** magazine every Friday.

A Circle the words that fit the definitions.

1. to be or live

   a. instruct   b. notice   c. include   d. exist

2. a person who invites guests

   a. safety   b. host   c. custom   d. fact

3. relating to a single person, place, thing, etc.

   a. particular   b. typical   c. weekly   d. nearly

4. to say how two things are similar and different

   a. encourage   b. compare   c. allow   d. chase

5. an announcement that something will happen

   a. list   b. custom   c. notice   d. safety

B Choose and write the correct words for the blanks.

chase	notice	safety	generally	typical	fact

1. risk   ≠ _____   2. follow   = _____

3. ignore   ≠ _____   4. truth   = _____

5. unusual ≠ _____   6. commonly = _____

C Circle the words that best fit the sentences.

1. Greg encouraged | chased me to try hard every day.

2. We have nearly | generally arrived at the airport.

3. Math class is since | unlike art class.

4. Her family has many interesting birthday notices | customs .

5. Lisa instructs | includes kindergarten students during summer.

6. They have a generally | weekly meeting every Monday.

D **Choose the correct words to complete the sentences.**

1. My parents _____ me to go camping with my friend.

   a. chased   b. compared   c. allowed   d. existed

2. Susan has a _____ of items to buy at the store.

   a. list   b. fact   c. notice   d. safety

3. It has been raining _____ this morning.

   a. particular   b. since   c. generally   d. nearly

4. Mammals _____ humans and monkeys.

   a. instruct   b. notice   c. encourage   d. include

5. It is a _____ that the Earth goes around the sun.

   a. fact   b. safety   c. host   d. custom

E **Read the passage. Then, write T for true or F for false.**

Tina is preparing to take a trip to Italy. Her parents are **allowing** her to go there with her friend. However, they are **encouraging** her to prepare for the trip. They are **instructing** her about **safety** rules. They also told her to make a **list** of the items she needs.

In **fact**, Tina has been preparing for the trip **since** last winter. She has **weekly** meetings with her friend to discuss the trip. **Generally**, they talk about the items they plan to bring with them. But they also talk about Italian **customs**. Some of them are different from the **customs** in their own country. One **particular custom** Tina **noticed** is that Italians often get very close to people when they speak. She thinks that will be difficult to get used to.

1. Tina and her parents are taking a trip to Italy.   _____

2. Tina's friend told her to make a list of items she needs.   _____

3. Tina has weekly meetings to talk about the trip.   _____

4. Italian customs are not like customs in Tina's country.   _____

1 adopt
[ədápt]

v. to accept or take as one's own
adopt a child
→ The couple wants to **adopt** a child soon.

2 attempt
[ətémpt]

v. to try to do something
n. the act of trying to do something
attempt to → He will **attempt** to set a new record.
make an attempt → Please make an **attempt** to improve.

3 chief
[tʃiːf]

n. the leader of a group of people   (syn) boss
adj. most important
police chief → The police **chief** will make his decision soon.
chief problem → His **chief** problem is he has no money.

4 chore
[tʃɔːr]

n. a small job to do at home   (syn) task
do one's chores
→ Do your **chores** before you play outside.

5 determine
[ditɜ́ːrmin]

v. to discover the facts about something; to make a decision
determine a cause → He tried to **determine** the cause of the fire.
determine that → I **determined** that it was a good idea.

6 develop
[divéləp]
n. development

v. to create something or to make it grow bigger
develop into
→ A tadpole will **develop** into a frog.

7 disappear
[dìsəpíər]

v. to stop being seen   (ant) appear
disappear from view
→ The airplane **disappeared** from view.

8 impress
[imprés]
adj. impressive

v. to have a strong effect on a person   (syn) amaze
impress someone
→ He **impressed** the audience with his singing.

9 inform
[infɔ́ːrm]
n. information

v. to give a person knowledge or news
inform about
→ He **informed** us about the bad news.

10 memorize
[méməràiz]
n. memory

v. to learn something by heart   (syn) remember
memorize a number
→ The girl **memorized** her parents' phone numbers.

11 method
[méθəd]

n. a way of doing something
perfect method
→ He has the perfect **method** for baking cookies.

12 owner
[óunər]

n. the person that something belongs to
owner of
→ Who is the **owner** of the red car?

13 precious
[préʃəs]

adj. of high price or value   [syn] expensive   [ant] cheap
precious metal
→ Gold and silver are **precious** metals.

14 produce
[prədjú:s]
n. product

v. to make or create   [ant] destroy
produce cars
→ This factory **produces** 100 cars each day.

15 recognize
[rékəgnàiz]

v. to identify or see something one knows
recognize someone
→ I **recognized** my old friend at once.

16 reflect
[riflékt]

v. to make an image of something
reflect an image
→ Mirrors are able to **reflect** images.

17 spot
[spɑt]

n. a small, round mark
v. to see or notice
ink spot → There is an ink **spot** on your shirt.
spot someone → She hopes to **spot** her friend in the crowd.

18 survive
[sərváiv]

v. to stay alive, often in a dangerous situation   [syn] live   [ant] die
survive a crash
→ Several people **survived** the plane crash.

19 tool
[tu:l]

n. equipment a person can hold with a hand
use a tool
→ He used several **tools** to build the house.

20 value
[vǽlju:]
adj. valuable

n. how much something costs
high value
→ That gold necklace has a high **value**.

A   **Circle the correct definitions for the given words.**

1. determine
   a. to make a decision
   c. to see or notice
   b. to accept or take as one's own
   d. to make or create

2. spot
   a. a small job to do at home
   c. a small, round mark
   b. a way of doing something
   d. the leader of a group of people

3. inform
   a. to make an image of something
   c. to learn something by heart
   b. to stop being seen
   d. to give a person knowledge or news

4. attempt
   a. how much something costs
   c. a small job to do at home
   b. the act of trying to do something
   d. the person that something belongs to

B   **Circle the two words in each group that are opposites.**

1. a. die   b. survive   c. reflect   d. impress

2. a. inform   b. adopt   c. produce   d. destroy

3. a. spot   b. precious   c. cheap   d. memorize

4. a. disappear b. recognize   c. attempt   d. appear

C   **Circle the words that best fit the sentences.**

1. The lake is reflecting | memorizing the trees in the water.

2. The scientist wants to survive | develop a new machine.

3. Mary has to finish her spots | chores at home now.

4. The chief | value of the village is the oldest man.

5. She does not disappear | recognize the man in the picture.

6. A hammer and a screwdriver are both tools | owners .

D **Choose the correct words to complete the sentences.**

1. He has a unique _____ of painting pictures.

    a. chief   b. spot   c. chore   d. method

2. The _____ of that broken item is very low.

    a. owner   b. tool   c. spot   d. value

3. He is trying to _____ everyone's name.

    a. disappear   b. memorize   c. survive   d. reflect

4. The player _____ us by scoring two goals.

    a. impressed   b. recognized   c. determined   d. produced

5. The couple plan to _____ a baby boy.

    a. attempt   b. develop   c. adopt   d. inform

E **Read the passage. Then, fill in the blanks.**

Samantha had a big problem. She never listened to her parents. She did not do her **chores** at home. She did not study at school either. She did not want to do anything at all. Then, one day, her friend Greg talked to her.

Greg **determined** that Samantha had a problem. He **informed** her that she was not **impressing** anyone with her actions. He told her that life was **precious**. If she wanted her life to have **value**, she needed to change her actions. Samantha **adopted** Greg's ideas. She knew he was right. Suddenly, the old Samantha **disappeared**. A new Samantha appeared. She started doing her **chores**. She **memorized** her lessons and studied hard. She **attempted** to be the best daughter for her parents.

1. The old Samantha did not do her _____ or listen to her parents.

2. Greg said Samantha was not _____ anyone.

3. Samantha _____ the ideas Greg had.

4. Samantha changed and _____ to be a good daughter.

A Choose and write the correct words for the definitions.

reflect	beauty	bitter	practical
unlike	exist	attempt	adapt

1. the quality of looking good to the eye ➡ _____

2. the act of trying to do something ➡ _____

3. to change something so it fits better ➡ _____

4. to be or live ➡ _____

5. to make an image of something ➡ _____

6. having an unpleasant taste ➡ _____

7. realistic or being useful ➡ _____

8. different or not equal ➡ _____

B Circle the words that are the most similar to the underlined words.

1. He always remains <u>quiet</u> during emergencies.
 a. aware   b. raw   c. smooth   d. calm

2. The dog is <u>following</u> the deer in the forest.
 a. including   b. noticing   c. chasing   d. comparing

3. The <u>main</u> problem is that we have no money.
 a. principal   b. common   c. valuable   d. ancient

4. She <u>responded</u> to his question at once.
 a. supplied   b. applied   c. appointed   d. replied

5. The magic trick <u>amazed</u> everyone in the audience.
 a. adopted   b. impressed   c. reflected   d. informed

C Choose the correct forms of the words to complete the sentences.

1. It is good to do regular | regularly exercise.

2. What is the value | valuable of that gold ring?

3. The storage room is very dirt | dirty now.

4. She is reading the conclude | conclusion of the report now.

5. The teachers often encourage | encouragement us to study hard.

D Complete the sentences with the words in the box.

1. His father will _____ for a job at a car company.

2. We all _____ when the show finished.

3. One of his _____ is to clean his bedroom every day.

4. I _____ it is okay to wait a few minutes.

5. She has not eaten anything _____ last night.

chores

clapped

since

apply

suppose

E Write the correct phrases in the blanks.

poured a drink	in cash	ancient history
perfect method	supply food	not nearly

1. Farmers _____ to people in cities and towns.

2. Don _____ for each of his guests.

3. The weather in spring is _____ hot enough.

4. Some people prefer to pay for items _____ .

5. This is the _____ to solve the problem.

6. _____ includes the study of Egypt.

F **Circle the mistakes. Then, write the correct sentences.**

1. We like to discussion different topics with our friends.

   ➡ _____

2. It takes a short time to product that item.

   ➡ _____

3. Alice was appointment the leader of the group.

   ➡ _____

4. He hopes to discovery a cure for the disease soon.

   ➡ _____

5. Her parents allowance her to play games on weekends.

   ➡ _____

G **Complete the crossword puzzle.**

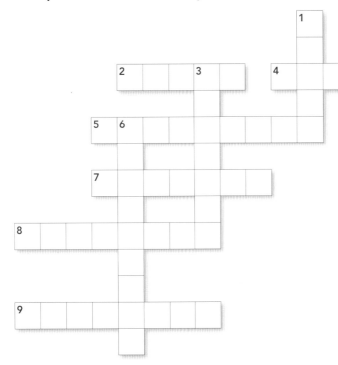

Across

2. to be or live
4. the rules that people must follow
5. to make a decision
7. how good or bad something is
8. very useful or important
9. a person who buys goods or services

Down

1. having knowledge
3. to stay alive, often in a dangerous situation
6. the act of teaching or learning

H **Read the passage. Then, answer the questions below.**

Education in Ancient Times

In **ancient** times, **education** was much different than today. People used various **methods** to **instruct** others. For example, there were not many schools in the past. Instead, **wealthy** people found an **expert** on a topic. Then, they paid him **cash** and studied with him. The teacher was often a **scholar**. He would give **lectures**. The students learned important **facts** from him. The students often tried to **memorize** the information they learned.

Students had **regular** classes with their teachers. They often had classes outdoors. The teachers would tell them to **notice** everything they saw. This **included** plants, animals, and other people. The **quality** of **education** in the past was high. It was **unusual** compared to today. But students could learn a lot. They considered their time with their teachers **valuable**. So they **generally** studied hard.

1. What is the passage mainly about?

   a. how people learned in ancient times

   b. why education is so important

   c. where most people studied in the past

   d. what topics people used to study

2. What kinds of people often studied with experts?

   a. young people   b. smart people

   c. wealthy people   d. old people

3. How did the students often learn the information they studied?

   a. They did experiments.   b. They memorized it.

   c. They wrote it down.   d. They talked to their friends about it.

4. How did scholars often teach their students?

   ➡ _____

5. What did teachers tell their students to notice?

   ➡ _____

1 appreciate
[əpríːʃièit]

v. to be thankful for

appreciate one's advice

→ I really **appreciate** your advice.

2 backward
[bǽkwərd]

adv. toward the rear or back   (ant) forward

look backward

→ You should look **backward** sometimes.

3 concern
[kənsə́ːrn]

n. a feeling of worry

v. to worry about someone

big concern → Making enough money is my big **concern**.

concern someone → What **concerns** you these days?

4 connect
[kənékt]

n. connection

v. to join or fasten together   (syn) link   (ant) separate

connect with

→ **Connect** the two parts with glue.

5 consider
[kənsídər]

adj. considerate

v. to think about very much

consider carefully

→ Please **consider** my offer carefully.

6 demand
[dimǽnd]

v. to ask for something as if it is one's right

demand payment

→ The manager **demanded** payment at once.

7 disappoint
[dìsəpɔ́int]

v. not to carry out someone's wish or desire   (syn) upset

disappoint someone

→ He tried not to **disappoint** his parents.

8 emotion
[imóuʃən]

n. a strong feeling such as love or hate

feel emotion

→ People are able to feel different **emotions**.

9 hesitate
[hézitèit]

v. to wait to act for a short period of time   (syn) pause

hesitate for a moment

→ Mary **hesitated** for a moment before asking.

10 insult
[insʌ́lt][ínsult]

v. to say something rude or upsetting

n. a rude or upsetting comment

insult someone → Please do not **insult** my friend.

ignore an insult → Joe ignored the **insults** they made.

11 measure
[méʒər]

v. to determine a length, weight, amount, etc.
measure a distance
→ Let's **measure** the distance from this point to that one.

12 option
[ápʃən]

n. a choice
have options
→ We have several **options** to choose from.

13 persuade
[pərswéid]

v. to get a person to do something
fail to persuade
→ Jack failed to **persuade** Martin to see the movie.

14 promise
[prámis]

v. to say that one will do something
n. a statement that one will do something
promise to → Please **promise** to help me tomorrow.
keep a promise → I always keep my **promises**.

15 relative
[rélətiv]

n. a member of one's family
meet one's relative
→ I usually meet my **relatives** on Christmas.

16 scene
[siːn]

n. the place where something happens   syn site
scene of
→ The police are at the **scene** of the crime.

17 selfish
[sélfiʃ]

adj. not willing to share with others
selfish man
→ The **selfish** man had no friends.

18 shy
[ʃai]

adj. being quiet or not likely to speak   ant confident
feel shy
→ Irene felt **shy** when everyone looked at her.

19 sincere
[sinsíər]
adv. sincerely

adj. real and honest   syn true   ant false
sincere apology
→ Harry gave a **sincere** apology to his mother.

20 whisper
[wíspər]

v. to speak in a low voice   ant shout
n. something said in a low voice
whisper softly → You should **whisper** softly in the library.
in a whisper → He is speaking in a **whisper**.

A **Match the words with their definitions.**

1. consider •   • a. to ask for something as if it is one's right

2. whisper •   • b. toward the rear or back

3. relative •   • c. something said in a low voice

4. demand •   • d. to determine a length, weight, amount, etc.

5. selfish •   • e. to get a person to do something

6. backward •   • f. not willing to share with others

7. persuade •   • g. to think about very much

8. measure •   • h. a member of one's family

B **Write S for synonym or A for antonym next to each pair or words.**

1. _____ scene – site   2. _____ shy – confident

3. _____ connect – separate   4. _____ disappoint – upset

5. _____ sincere – false   6. _____ hesitate – pause

C **Circle the words that best fit the sentences.**

1. You should not hesitate | insult other people.

2. I made a whisper | promise to help my parents.

3. She decided to take the second option | whisper .

4. They were concerned | demanded about her health.

5. Happiness is a very common ralative | emotion .

6. Jane appreciates | persuades all the help everyone gave her.

106

D **Choose the correct words to complete the sentences.**

1. The boy is _____ and hates sharing his toys.

   a. shy   b. sincere   c. backward   d. selfish

2. She _____ her friend by telling a lie.

   a. whispered   b. disappointed   c. considered   d. measured

3. Do not _____ if you have a good chance.

   a. hesitate   b. appreciate   c. persuade   d. insult

4. You can _____ the two pieces easily.

   a. concern   b. promise   c. connect   d. demand

5. There is a lot of _____ about the illness.

   a. emotion   b. concern   c. relative   d. scene

E **Read the passage. Then, write T for true or F for false.**

Some people are very **selfish**. They have **concern** only for themselves. These people are often unable to **connect** with others. For example, they often **demand** that people do certain things for them. But they refuse to help those people in return. They simply do not **consider** other people's **emotions**. They may even **insult** people who do not want to help them. These **selfish** people typically have very bad manners.

However, many people are very **sincere**. They **appreciate** any help that others provide for them. They also keep their **promises**. So it is easy for them to **persuade** others to do favors for them. In fact, most people do not **hesitate** to assist **sincere** people. As a result, **sincere** people get along with others better than **selfish** people do.

1. Selfish people can connect well with others.   _____

2. Selfish people do not consider others' emotions.   _____

3. Sincere people appreciate the help others provide for them.   _____

4. People usually hesitate to help sincere individuals.   _____

1 area
[éəriə]

n. a certain place or part   (syn) region
local area
➡ John knows the entire local **area**.

2 base
[beis]

n. the lowest part of something
strong base
➡ The statue has a very strong **base**.

3 beg
[beg]
n. beggar

v. to ask for something   (syn) request
beg for money
➡ The poor man **begged** people for money.

4 bottom
[bátəm]

n. the lowest part of something   (syn) base   (ant) top
bottom of
➡ They are waiting at the **bottom** of the hill.

5 continent
[kántinənt]

n. a very large mass of land, such as Asia or Africa
cross a continent
➡ It can take days to cross a **continent**.

6 crowd
[kraud]

n. a group of people in one place
crowd of people
➡ There was a big **crowd** of people at the park.

7 distance
[dístəns]
adj. distant

n. the amount of space between two things
short distance
➡ My home is a short **distance** from school.

8 divide
[diváid]

v. to separate something into parts   (syn) cut   (ant) unite
divide into
➡ **Divide** the pizza into eight slices.

9 familiar
[fəmílər]

adj. commonly known or seen   (ant) unknown
familiar place
➡ Karen likes eating at **familiar** places.

10 fence
[fens]

n. a structure that surrounds a piece of land   (syn) wall
high fence
➡ There is a high **fence** all around his land.

11 ideal
[aidí(ː)əl]

adj. being perfect   *syn* best   *ant* worst
ideal opportunity
→ We have an **ideal** opportunity to become rich.

12 illegal
[ilíːgəl]

adj. against the law   *ant* legal
illegal act
→ You should not do any **illegal** acts.

13 official
[əfíʃəl]

n. a person elected or appointed to a position
adj. done by someone in authority
government official → The president is a government **official**.
official request → He made an **official** request to the mayor.

14 population
[pàpjuléiʃən]

n. the number of people in a certain area
local population
→ The local **population** is around 10,000 people.

15 president
[prézidənt]

n. the elected leader of a country, company, etc.
elect a president
→ Koreans elect a new **president** every five years.

16 slave
[sleiv]

n. a person who is owned by another   *ant* free man
become a slave
→ Many people became **slaves** in the past.

17 species
[spíːʃiːz]

n. a plant or animal group that has similar features
animal species
→ There are many animal **species** living here.

18 tribe
[traib]

n. a group of people who are often related or closely connected
Native American tribe
→ Native American **tribes** have strong traditions.

19 unit
[júːnit]

n. a single person, thing, or group
basic unit
→ The basic **unit** of society is the family.

20 worth
[wɜːrθ]

prep. having a certain value of
n. excellent in character or quality
be worth → The painting is **worth** a fortune.
of worth → Tim is a man of **worth**.

A Circle the words that fit the definitions.

1. the amount of space between two things

   a. distance   b. continent   c. bottom   d. area

2. a plant or animal group that has similar features

   a. species   b. president   c. unit   d. fence

3. done by someone in authority

   a. illegal   b. ideal   c. official   d. familiar

4. the number of people in a certain area

   a. continent   b. population   c. worth   d. tribe

5. a group of people in one place

   a. unit   b. slave   c. base   d. crowd

B Choose and write the correct words for the blanks.

slave	familiar	fence	area	ideal	bottom

1. unknown ≠ _____

2. wall = _____

3. base = _____

4. free man ≠ _____

5. region = _____

6. worst ≠ _____

C Circle the words that best fit the sentences.

1. The diamond necklace is an item of great distance | worth .

2. Tom begged | divided for help, but nobody gave him any.

3. The Asian president | continent is the biggest in the world.

4. It is official | illegal to steal possessions from others.

5. There are some lost tribes | bottoms in the Amazon Rainforest.

6. The landmark is familiar | ideal to many people.

D **Choose the correct words to complete the sentences.**

1. The class was _____ into groups of four students each.

   a. begged   b. ideal   c. divided   d. illegal

2. Leslie wants to become the _____ of her company.

   a. continent   b. president   c. crowd   d. distance

3. The _____ of the pyramid is as long as a soccer field.

   a. base   b. worth   c. tribe   d. population

4. Several plant _____ grow in this forest.

   a. fences   b. areas   c. species   d. slaves

5. One _____ of measurement is the meter.

   a. bottom   b. distance   c. official   d. unit

E **Read the passage. Then, fill in the blanks.**

    The United States is located on the North American **continent**. It has a **population** of more than 330,000,000 people. The **president** is the leader of the country.

    In the past, the United States did not exist. Instead, many Native American **tribes** lived in the **area**. Then, Europeans began to sail across the Atlantic Ocean. Large **crowds** of people traveled great **distances** to get there. Many people went to America, and the land became **familiar** to them. For some people, America was an **ideal** place. There were many kinds of plant and animal **species**. As the **population** grew, people moved west. The Native American **tribes** also had to leave their homelands. They searched for new **areas** to live in. Many had to travel far to find new homes for themselves.

1. The _____ of the United States is over 330,000,000 people.

2. Many Native American _____ used to live in America.

3. Many Europeans traveled great _____ to get to America.

4. There were many _____ of plants and animals in America.

1	**bare** [beər]	*adj.* without clothes or covering bare feet → We walked in our **bare** feet at the beach.
2	**beard** [biərd]	*n.* the hair on a man's face thick beard → My father sometimes grows a thick **beard**.
3	**cell** [sel]	*n.* the basic unit of all living things blood cell → Red blood **cells** carry oxygen.
4	**chest** [tʃest]	*n.* the front of the body between the neck and the stomach chest pain → The man is suffering from **chest** pains.
5	**elbow** [élbou]	*n.* the joint where the arm bends bend one's elbow → People are able to bend their **elbows**.
6	**exactly** [igzǽktli] *adj.* exact	*adv.* in a precise way syn correctly ant wrongly remember exactly → David remembers **exactly** where he lived.
7	**footprint** [fútprìnt]	*n.* a mark on a surface made by a foot leave a footprint → His dirty feet left **footprints** on the floor.
8	**huge** [hjuːdʒ]	*adj.* very large ant tiny huge animal → The dinosaurs were **huge** animals.
9	**imitate** [ímitèit]	*v.* to copy someone or something imitate someone → Kelly is good at **imitating** her father.
10	**infect** [infékt]	*v.* to affect a person or animal with a disease infect with → Mary was **infected** with the flu virus.

11 jaw
[dʒɔː]

n. the two bones that form the mouth
break one's jaw
→ Greg broke his **jaw** in a car accident.

12 lower
[lóuər]

v. to cause to go down or reduce   *ant* raise
adj. less high than
lower a flag → They **lower** the flag in the evening.
lower level → The store is on a **lower** level.

13 lung
[lʌŋ]

n. the body part that lets people breathe
lung disease
→ His grandfather is sick with a **lung** disease.

14 organic
[ɔːrgǽnik]
v. organize

adj. developing through natural growth
organic vegetable
→ My mother only buys **organic** vegetables.

15 position
[pəzíʃən]

n. a certain place or situation; the way someone is sitting or lying
good position → He found a good **position** for his new house.
comfortable position → You should rest in a comfortable **position**.

16 power
[páuər]
adj. powerful

n. the ability to do or act   *syn* strength
have power
→ Anna has the **power** to do anything she wants.

17 race
[reis]

n. a group of related people who look similar; a contest   *syn* competition
white race → Many Europeans belong to the white **race**.
running race → Eric came in first in the running **race**.

18 stomach
[stʌ́mək]

n. the body part that stores and breaks down food   *syn* belly
full stomach
→ After eating a lot, John had a full **stomach**.

19 thumb
[θʌm]

n. the short, inner finger on the hand
be all thumbs
→ Ken is all **thumbs**, so he often knocks things over.

20 whole
[houl]

adj. full or complete   *syn* total
whole game
→ He was tired after playing the **whole** game.

Unit 23

113

A Match the words with their definitions.

1. infect •
2. lower •
3. cell •
4. position •
5. imitate •
6. bare •
7. organic •
8. jaw •

• a. to copy someone or something
• b. developing through natural growth
• c. to cause to go down or reduce
• d. the way someone is sitting or lying
• e. without clothes or covering
• f. to affect a person or animal with a disease
• g. the two bones that form the mouth
• h. the basic unit of all living things

B Circle the two words in each group that have the same meaning.

1. a. strength   b. position   c. race   d. power

2. a. imitate   b. exactly   c. correctly   d. infect

3. a. total   b. whole   c. organic   d. bare

4. a. elbow   b. thumb   c. stomach   d. belly

C Circle the words that best fit the sentences.

1. The hunter found some lion footprints | elbows on the jungle floor.

2. The students had a power | race to the school's front gate.

3. Some men have beards | thumbs on their faces these days.

4. You need your lungs | jaw to help you breathe.

5. Dinosaurs were whole | huge animals that lived in the past.

6. The man has many muscles in his position | chest .

D **Choose the correct words to complete the sentences.**

1. You should press the button with your _____.

    a. stomach   b. cell   c. footprint   d. thumb

2. I broke my _____ when I fell down the stairs.

    a. position   b. elbow   c. beard   d. race

3. The motor does not have enough _____ to run.

    a. jaw   b. steals   c. chest   d. power

4. Monkeys often _____ people watching them.

    a. imitate   b. infect   c. lower   d. exactly

5. The _____ movie lasts for two hours.

    a. organic   b. bare   c. whole   d. huge

E **Read the passage. Then, write T for true or F for false.**

Each human has a head, two arms, and two legs. The arms are connected to the **chest**. The **elbow** connects the upper arm with the **lower** arm. Each hand has five fingers. We call the short, thick finger the **thumb**. As for the **lower** body, each person has two legs. The knee connects the upper leg with the **lower** leg.

While all humans have the same body parts, they do not all look **exactly** the same. For instance, there are many **races** of people on the Earth. Some are white, and some are black. In addition, some men have **beards** on their faces while others have **bare** faces. If people eat too much, they may have **huge stomachs**. But skinny people do not have **stomachs** that stick out.

1. The elbow connects the arm to the chest. _____

2. One of the fingers is called a thumb. _____

3. All humans look exactly the same. _____

4. Some men have beards while others have bare faces. _____

1 attract
[ətrǽkt]
n. attraction

v. to pull or draw toward something
attract someone
→ His performance **attracted** many people.

2 cart
[kɑːrt]

n. a small vehicle pushed or pulled by hand
shopping cart
→ I put the food in my shopping **cart**.

3 continue
[kəntínju(ː)]

v. to keep doing something
continue doing
→ Stella picked up her book and **continued** reading.

4 display
[displéi]

v. to show something to people   syn exhibit
n. an arrangement of things for people to look at
display clothes → The store **displays** clothes in its windows.
art display → We saw the art **display** at the museum.

5 electronic
[ilektránik]

adj. relating to items that run on electricity
electronic equipment
→ James will repair the **electronic** equipment.

6 flavor
[fléivər]

n. a certain taste
sweet flavor
→ The cupcakes have a very sweet **flavor**.

7 found
[faund]

v. to start an organization, school, etc.   syn establish
found a company
→ Mr. Thompson **founded** his company in 2002.

8 gift
[gift]

n. something given to a person   syn present
give a gift
→ People give **gifts** to others on their birthdays.

9 jewel
[dʒúːəl]
n. jewelry

n. a precious stone
expensive jewel
→ Lewis bought an expensive **jewel** for his wife.

10 mail
[meil]

n. letters or packages that are sent
v. to send a letter or package to someone
get mail → Janet got some **mail** this morning.
mail a letter → I will **mail** a letter to my parents.

11 metal
[métəl]

n. a hard substance like iron or gold
made of metal
→ This desk is made of **metal**.

12 object
[ábdʒekt]

n. anything that can be seen; the aim of a plan or action
missing object → Let's try to find the missing **object**.
main object → The main **object** is to win the game.

13 order
[ɔ́:rdər]

n. the way that things are arranged; a command
v. to ask for goods to be made or supplied
alphabetical order → Put the books in alphabetical **order**.
order food → She often **orders** food online.

14 owe
[ou]

v. to have to pay or pay back a person
owe money
→ Irene **owes** money to her friend.

15 pack
[pæk]

n. a group of things wrapped or tied together   (syn) box
pack of gum
→ There are five pieces in a **pack** of gum.

16 refuse
[rifjú:z]

v. to turn down or say no   (ant) accept
refuse help
→ The man **refused** help from his friends.

17 return
[ritɜ́:rn]

v. to give back or go back   (ant) leave
return home
→ My mom told me to **return** home by 6:00.

18 sample
[sǽmpl]

n. a small part of something to try   (syn) example
try a sample
→ She tried a **sample** before buying the food.

19 steal
[sti:l]
steal - stole - stolen

v. to take something without asking or paying for it
steal money
→ The thief **stole** money from the bank.

20 various
[vé(:)əriəs]
n. variety

adj. of different kinds   (ant) similar
various reasons
→ He refused to attend the meeting for **various** reasons.

A **Circle the words that fit the definitions.**

1. to pull or draw toward something

   a. return   b. owe   c. found   d. attract

2. a certain taste

   a. mail   b. flavor   c. jewel   d. pack

3. the way that things are arranged

   a. order   b. cart   c. metal   d. gift

4. anything that can be seen

   a. pack   b. display   c. object   d. sample

5. relating to items that run on electricity

   a. electronic   b. continue   c. various   d. steal

B **Write S for synonym or A for antonym next to each pair of words.**

1. _____ various – similar   2. _____ sample – example

3. _____ display – exhibit   4. _____ return – leave

5. _____ found – establish   6. _____ refuse – accept

C **Circle the words that best fit the sentences.**

1. There is an expensive mail | jewel in the gold ring.

2. It is wrong to steal | continue items from other people.

3. Stuart bought a flavor | pack of playing cards at the store.

4. He mailed | attracted a box to his friend yesterday.

5. Doug owes | refuses his friend fifteen dollars.

6. Janet gave her sister a display | gift on her birthday.

D **Choose the correct words to complete the sentences.**

1. _____ such as gold and silver are worth a lot of money.

    a. Displays   b. Flavors   c. Packs   d. Metals

2. She put her luggage on a _____ in the airport.

    a. mail   b. flavor   c. cart   d. jewel

3. The story _____ in another book.

    a. continues   b. steals   c. refuses   d. owes

4. Ben will _____ the game he borrowed to his friend.

    a. order   b. return   c. attract   d. steal

5. Ms. Wright wants to _____ a new organization this year.

    a. display   b. found   c. mail   d. refuse

E **Read the passage. Then, fill in the blanks.**

These days, there are many ways for people to go shopping. Some people prefer visiting big stores. They get shopping **carts** and walk up and down the aisles. They enjoy looking at **various objects** for sale. Some love the **displays** of items in stores. Good **displays** can **attract** many shoppers. **Electronic objects** and **jewels** are popular items at some stores.

Other people prefer to shop online. They **order various** items on websites. For them, shopping online is convenient. However, sometimes items arrive in the **mail** very slowly. And some online stores **refuse** to let shoppers **return** goods. Shoppers also cannot try any **samples** of items they **order**. So that can be difficult at times. Still, people **continue** to shop online because they can do that anytime of the day.

1. Shoppers like looking at various _____ for sale.

2. Electronic items and _____ are popular at some stores.

3. Some online stores refuse to let people _____ goods.

4. Online stores are convenient, so people _____ to use them.

1	**behind** [biháind]	*prep.* at or toward the back stand behind → Amy is standing **behind** her friend.
2	**bubble** [bʌ́bl]	*n.* a ball of gas in a liquid blow bubbles → The children love to blow **bubbles**.
3	**certain** [sɜ́:rtən] *adv.* certainly	*adj.* sure and free from doubt (syn) confident for certain → I will arrive tonight for **certain**.
4	**code** [koud]	*n.* a system of letters or symbols for secret messages Morse Code → People use Morse **Code** for telegraph messages.
5	**dare** [deər]	*v.* to be brave enough to try something (syn) challenge dare to → No one **dared** to go into the house at night.
6	**enemy** [énəmi]	*n.* someone who wants fight against another person (ant) friend fight one's enemy → They are fighting their **enemy** in a war.
7	**escape** [iskéip]	*v.* to get away from escape from jail → Two thieves **escaped** from the jail.
8	**fortunately** [fɔ́:rtʃənətli]	*adv.* in a lucky manner (syn) luckily (ant) unfortunately quite fortunately → Quite **fortunately**, nobody was hurt.
9	**guess** [ges]	*v.* to try to figure out something (syn) suppose *n.* an attempt to figure out something guess an answer → He **guessed** the right answer at once. make a guess → She made a **guess** about the price.
10	**handle** [hǽndl]	*n.* something made to be grabbed *v.* to deal with a situation or problem metal handle → She is holding on to the metal **handle**. handle a problem → I think Tina can **handle** the problem.

11 joy
[dʒɔi]

n. a feeling of great happiness   syn delight

feel joy

→ Steve felt **joy** when he got some birthday presents.

12 length
[leŋkθ]

adj. long

n. the measure of something from one point to another

in length

→ The fish is 30 centimeters in **length**.

13 magic
[mǽdʒik]

adj. magical

n. the power to make impossible things happen

do magic

→ Harry Potter is able to do **magic**.

14 monster
[mánstər]

n. a creature that is usually large and ugly

fight a monster

→ In the story, the hero must fight many **monsters**.

15 original
[ərídʒənəl]

adv. originally

adj. new or different from everything else; existing first

original story → The author's **original** story became popular

original receipt → I need to see the **original** receipt.

16 perform
[pərfɔ́ːrm]

n. performance

v. to carry out, do, or act

perform an experiment

→ The scientists will **perform** an experiment.

17 release
[rilíːs]

v. to let go or free   ant capture

release a prisoner

→ They **released** the prisoner from jail.

18 source
[sɔːrs]

n. the place where something comes from   syn origin

source of

→ The **source** of the river is a small stream on a mountain.

19 treasure
[tréʒər]

n. valuable things such as gold or jewels

find treasure

→ They hope to find some **treasure** in the cave.

20 war
[wɔːr]

n. fighting between two or more countries   syn battle   ant peace

win a war

→ The king won the **war** against his enemy.

A **Match the words with their definitions.**

1. guess •   • a. to try to figure out something

2. source •   • b. new or different from everything else

3. joy •   • c. to get away from

4. magic •   • d. to be brave enough to try something

5. escape •   • e. a feeling of great happiness

6. dare •   • f. something made to be grabbed

7. handle •   • g. the power to make impossible things happen

8. original •   • h. the place where something comes from

B **Circle the two words in each group that are opposites.**

1. a. perform   b. dare   c. release   d. capture

2. a. treasure   b. war   c. monster   d. peace

3. a. friend   b. enemy   c. magic   d. source

4. a. fortunately   b. certain   c. unfortunately d. original

C **Circle the words that best fit the sentences.**

1. We are original | certain it is going to snow tonight.

2. The spy used a code | joy to write the letter.

3. Can you release | guess the correct answer?

4. The length | bubble of the field is fifty meters.

5. The actors will escape | perform a play for the audience.

6. The dragon is guarding a huge pile of treasure | magic .

D **Choose the correct words to complete the sentences.**

1. There is someone standing right _____ John.
   a. original   b. certain   c. fortunately   d. behind

2. The story has _____ like trolls and goblins in it.
   a. joys   b. monsters   c. codes   d. wars

3. The police _____ the man since he was innocent.
   a. escaped   b. performed   c. handled   d. released

4. There are some _____ in the water now.
   a. guesses   b. codes   c. bubbles   d. lengths

5. The _____ between the two countries lasted for five years.
   a. war   b. treasure   c. source   d. magic

E **Read the passage. Then, write T for true or F for false.**

> Every day after school, some students experience **joy**. They **escape** to a special place. There, they experience stories with **magic** and **monsters**. They learn about **enemies** and **wars** in the past. They find out about **treasures** people discovered, too. Where are the students going? They are going to the school library. And they are reading books.
>
> The librarian is busy, but she can **handle** all the students. She **guesses** the books they will enjoy. So she recommends some books to some students. The **lengths** of some books are short while others are long. Sometimes after the students read a book, they **perform** scenes from it for their friends. The students really love the library. **Fortunately**, there are many books for them to read there.

1. The students escape to a place after school.   _____

2. The students are reading books at the public library.   _____

3. The librarian guesses which books students will enjoy.   _____

4. Students always perform scenes from books they read.   _____

A Choose and write the correct words for the definitions.

owe	cell	relative	monster
continent	bubble	position	emotion

1. a very large mass of land, such as Asia or Africa ➡ _____

2. the basic unit of all living things ➡ _____

3. a strong feeling such as love or hate ➡ _____

4. to have to pay or pay back a person ➡ _____

5. a ball of gas in a liquid ➡ _____

6. a creature that is usually large and ugly ➡ _____

7. the way someone is sitting or lying ➡ _____

8. a member of one's family ➡ _____

B Circle the words that are the most similar to the underlined words.

1. You must link these two wires together.
   a. promise   b. measure   c. demand   d. connect

2. John was the winner of the competition.
   a. cell   b. race   c. footprint   d. thumb

3. She challenged him to try to climb the mountain.
   a. performed   b. dared   c. handled   d. released

4. Let's cut the pizza into slices.
   a. divide   b. beg   c. disappoint   d. consider

5. The museum is exhibiting many items.
   a. stealing   b. founding   c. returning   d. displaying

C Choose the correct forms of the words to complete the sentences.

1. There is a great distant | distance between Japan and Canada.

2. Lights can attract | attraction some insects at night.

3. He is sincere | sincerely in his desire to learn the piano.

4. Eric will performance | perform a magic trick on stage.

5. The engine lacks the power | powerful to give energy to the entire house.

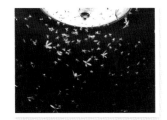

D Complete the sentences with the words in the box.

1. I _____ myself by failing the test.

2. It takes him two weeks to grow a full _____.

3. _____, it did not snow too much.

4. That is a rare _____ of insect.

5. The students want to _____ a new club at school.

| fortunately |
| disappointed |
| found |
| beard |
| species |

E Write the correct phrases in the blanks.

| in a whisper | organic vegetables | chest pains |
| standing behind | return home | local area |

1. Jason is _____ his big brother.

2. The _____ has lots of forests and lakes.

3. The farmer grows many _____.

4. I _____ by bus every day.

5. They spoke _____ inside the movie theater.

6. See a doctor if you have any _____.

F **Circle the mistakes. Then, write the correct sentences.**

1. I will carefully considerate the best thing to do.

   ➡ _____

2. There are variety problems with the new machine.

   ➡ _____

3. She told me exact what to do.

   ➡ _____

4. The long of the boat is around six meters.

   ➡ _____

5. Jane is certainly she can solve the puzzle.

   ➡ _____

G **Complete the crossword puzzle.**

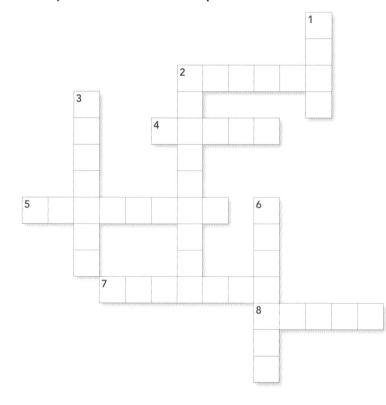

Across

2. a certain taste
4. having a certain value of
5. valuable things such as gold or jewels
7. to copy someone or something
8. to try to figure out something

Down

1. a small vehicle pushed or pulled by hand
2. a mark on a surface made by a foot
3. to worry about someone
6. against the law

H **Read the passage. Then, answer the questions below.**

Robots

Nowadays, robot workers are **familiar** to people. They **perform various** tasks. For example, they **connect objects** and **handle** machines at factories. Some push **carts** at malls. Some **measure** the **distances** of places. And people often **order** food from robot waiters. Robot curators also explain **displays** at museums. They work in many **areas** of human society.

Robots are **electronic objects** made of **metal**. In the past, some had simple parts like a face, a **chest**, arms, and legs. Nowadays, some have more detailed parts like a **jaw**, **elbows**, and even **thumbs**. They even have **various emotions exactly** like humans. But their **emotions** are not real. They are **imitating** humans thanks to their programming.

Some people think robots might become humans' **enemies**. Then, humans might become robots' **slaves**. **Fortunately**, scientists believe that will never happen.

1. What is the passage mainly about?
   a. how people make robots
   b. where robots work
   c. why people invented robots
   d. what robots do and look like

2. What do robots NOT do?
   a. They work in factories.   b. They help out at museums.
   c. They cook food for people.   d. They connect objects.

3. What did robots have in the past?
   a. elbows   b. arms
   c. thumbs   d. a jaw

4. What is true about robots' emotions?

   ➡ _____

5. What do some people think robots might do?

   ➡ _____

1	**blend** [blend] *n.* blender	*v.* to mix two or more things together (syn) combine blend ingredients → **Blend** the ingredients with a mixer.	
2	**cave** [keiv]	*n.* a hole in the ground or in a mountain explore a cave → It can be dangerous to explore a **cave**.	
3	**dew** [dju:]	*n.* small drops of water that collect on the ground at night covered with dew → The grass is all covered with **dew**.	
4	**dive** [daiv]	*v.* to jump into the water with one's head first dive in → Harry loves to **dive** in the water.	
5	**entrance** [éntrəns] *v.* enter	*n.* a place where a person can go into something (syn) door (ant) exit main entrance → Everyone used the main **entrance** of the building.	
6	**flight** [flait] *v.* fly	*n.* a trip on a plane; the act of flying in the air catch a flight → I must hurry to catch my **flight**. achieve flight → The Wright brothers achieved **flight** in 1903.	
7	**grain** [grein]	*n.* a seed of a plant like rice or corn grain of → There are many **grains** of rice in the bowl.	
8	**ground** [graund]	*n.* the solid surface of the Earth (syn) land hard ground → The farmer must dig up the hard **ground**.	
9	**harbor** [há:rbər]	*n.* an area of water near land for ships to sail in sail into a harbor → The ship sailed into the **harbor** before the storm.	
10	**north** [nɔ:rθ] *adj.* northern	*n.* the direction to the left of the rising sun North America → The United States is in **North** America.	

11 planet
[plǽnit]

n. a large body that moves around the sun

large planet

→ Jupiter and Saturn are both large **planets**.

12 polar
[póulər]

adj. near the northern or southern ends of the Earth

polar region

→ The **polar** regions are often cold and snowy.

13 rare
[reər]

adv. rarely

adj. not common or hard to find   (syn) unusual   (ant) usual

rare stamp

→ My uncle likes to collect **rare** stamps.

14 root
[ru(:)t]

n. the part of a plant that grows underground

plant roots

→ Plant **roots** get nutrients and water from the soil.

15 seafood
[síːfùːd]

n. fish or shellfish that people eat as food

eat seafood

→ We plan to eat **seafood** for dinner tonight.

16 shell
[ʃel]

n. the hard outer covering of an animal

live in a shell

→ Clams and oysters live in **shells**.

17 shore
[ʃɔːr]

n. land next to a river, ocean, sea, or lake   (syn) coast

on the shore

→ The ship is lying on the **shore**.

18 southern
[sʌ́ðərn]

n. south

adj. in or from the south

southern state

→ The weather in **southern** states is very hot.

19 tomb
[tuːm]

n. a place where a person is buried   (syn) grave

family tomb

→ Chris was buried in his family **tomb** after he died.

20 universe
[júːnivɜːrs]

adj. universal

n. the whole of space and everything in it

entire universe

→ Nobody knows how big the entire **universe** is.

A Circle the words that fit the definitions.

1. the direction to the left of the rising sun

    a. grain   b. north   c. ground   d. universe

2. the part of a plant that grows underground

    a. dew   b. shell   c. root   d. cave

3. an area of water near land for ships to sail in

    a. entrance   b. seafood   c. shore   d. harbor

4. near the northern or southern ends of the Earth

    a. planet   b. rare   c. polar   d. shell

5. to jump into the water with one's head first

    a. dive   b. blend   c. tomb   d. flight

B Choose and write the correct words for the blanks.

rare	blend	entrance	tomb	shore	ground

1. coast   = _____

2. exit   ≠ _____

3. usual   ≠ _____

4. combine   = _____

5. land   = _____

6. grave   = _____

C Circle the words that best fit the sentences.

1. The farmer grows corn, wheat, and other planets | grains .

2. I will take a flight | harbor to Australia next week.

3. He is going to plant some seeds in the dew | ground .

4. Nobody knows how big the universe | seafood is.

5. We like to collect caves | shells at the beach.

6. They spent their vacation on the southern | rare islands.

D **Choose the correct words to complete the sentences.**

1. There are eight _____ in the solar system.
   a. shores   b. roots   c. harbors   d. planets

2. He enjoys eating _____ such as shrimp and lobster.
   a. caves   b. seafood   c. tombs   d. grains

3. A bear lives somewhere in that dark _____.
   a. shell   b. dew   c. flight   d. cave

4. That is a _____ coin, so it is worth a lot of money.
   a. rare   b. polar   c. southern   d. ground

5. _____ is on the grass early every morning.
   a. Entrance   b. North   c. Dew   d. Universe

E **Read the passage. Then, fill in the blanks.**

The **flight** was going across the Pacific Ocean. Suddenly, the airplane developed a problem and crashed in the water. The people on board were safe. They saw an island nearby and swam to it. When they got to **shore**, everyone fell down on the **ground** and rested.

For the next few days, the people explored the island. In the **southern** part, there were many fruit trees. To the **north**, they found a **harbor** with plenty of **seafood** and **shells**. One person found some **grain** growing in a field. They also discovered a **cave**, where they slept. At night, everyone looked up at the stars and **planets** in the sky. One day, a plane flew overhead. The people waved, and the pilot waved back at them. They were saved!

1. The people on the plane swam to _____.

2. There were fruit trees in the _____ part of the island.

3. The people got _____ and shells in the harbor.

4. At night, everyone slept in a _____ they found.

1

depend
[dipénd]

v. to rely on or trust someone

depend on

→ You can always **depend** on me.

2

die
[dai]

n. death

v. to stop living or no longer be alive   (ant) live

die of

→ The old man **died** of a heart attack.

3

emerge
[imɔ́:rdʒ]

n. emergency

v. to come into view   (syn) appear   (ant) disappear

emerge from

→ The moon **emerged** from behind the clouds.

4

except
[iksépt]

prep. not including

except for

→ Everyone **except** for Dave went on the trip.

5

fear
[fiər]

n. the feeling when one is afraid   (syn) horror

v. to be afraid of

fear of → Janet has a **fear** of heights.

fear someone → She **fears** that man with the gun.

6

force
[fɔ:rs]

v. to make a person do something

n. physical power

force to → The thief **forced** them to give him the money.

great force → It took great **force** to open the door.

7

god
[gad]

n. a being who has great powers

god of

→ Ares was the **god** of war in Greek mythology.

8

hide
[haid]

hide - hid - hidden

v. to prevent others from seeing oneself

hide from

→ The zebras are **hiding** from the lion.

9

justice
[dʒʌ́stis]

n. the quality of doing what is right   (syn) honesty

receive justice

→ He received **justice** by being sent to jail.

10

liberty
[líbərti]

n. freedom   (syn) independence

fight for liberty

→ The colonists are fighting for **liberty**.

11 movement
[mú:vmənt]
v. move

n. the act of producing motion
slow movement
→ He does his work with slow **movements**.

12 path
[pæθ]

n. a route or way somewhere   (syn) trail
walk on a path
→ Sue is walking on a **path** up a mountain.

13 plenty
[plénti]

n. a lot of or a full amount   (ant) little
plenty of
→ We have **plenty** of food for dinner.

14 poor
[puər]
n. poverty

adj. having little money or possessions   (ant) rich
poor man
→ The **poor** man has no money.

15 proverb
[prάvɜːrb]

n. a wise saying
old proverb
→ "Time is money" is an old **proverb**.

16 rent
[rent]
adj. rental

v. to pay money regularly to use something
n. money paid regularly to use something
rent a home → John's family **rents** their home.
pay rent → I pay **rent** on the first day of each month.

17 sense
[sens]
adj. sensitive

n. a feeling from outside the body
v. to become aware of something
sense of → Jane has a good **sense** of touch.
sense a problem → My mother is good at **sensing** problems.

18 stage
[steidʒ]

n. a raised platform for performers; a period of development
act on stage → Tim will act on **stage** in a play tonight.
adult stage → All insects have an adult **stage**.

19 sudden
[sΛdən]
adv. suddenly

adj. happening quickly or unexpectedly   (syn) rapid (ant) gradual
sudden noise
→ Everyone was surprised by the **sudden** noise.

20 tide
[taid]

n. the rising and falling of waters in oceans and seas
high tide
→ During high **tide**, the water level rises.

A **Circle the correct definitions for the given words.**

1. proverb

    a. a wise saying   b. a route or way somewhere

    c. physical power   d. a being who has great powers

2. justice

    a. the act of producing motion   b. freedom

    c. the feeling when one is afraid   d. the quality of doing what is right

3. hide

    a. to come into view   b. to prevent others from seeing oneself

    c. to be afraid of   d. to stop living or no longer be alive

4. depend

    a. to make a person do something   b. to come into view

    c. to rely on or trust someone   d. to become aware of something

B **Circle the two words in each group that have the same meaning.**

1. a. force   b. liberty   c. fear   d. independence

2. a. path   b. trail   c. justice   d. proverb

3. a. hide   b. depend   c. appear   d. emerge

4. a. sudden   b. poor   c. rapid   d. except

C **Circle the words that best fit the sentences.**

1. The ancient Romans worshiped many gods | movements .

2. Some people died | rented because of the typhoon.

3. Because he is sudden | poor , he has little money to spend.

4. Except | Poor for Mark, all the students got A's.

5. The actor got nervous when he stood on the justice | stage .

6. At low tide | liberty people can walk far from shore.

D **Choose the correct words to complete the sentences.**

1. We saw some _____ behind the trees in the forest.

   a. movement   b. justice   c. liberty   d. sense

2. I _____ there was a problem with the machine.

   a. depended   b. died   c. rented   d. sensed

3. It requires a lot of _____ to lift the stone.

   a. path   b. god   c. force   d. proverb

4. Do not _____ the storm even if there is lightning.

   a. emerge   b. hide   c. fear   d. rent

5. There is _____ of work for everyone to do.

   a. stage   b. plenty   c. tide   d. justice

E **Read the passage. Then, write T for true or F for false.**

In England in the 1600s, many people did not have **liberty**. They lived in **fear** of the government. They had beliefs in **God** that were different from those of others. The government wanted to **force** them to live a certain way. But these people refused and had to **hide**.

Then, there was a **sudden movement** of these people. Many sailed across the Atlantic Ocean. They went to America. There, they could live lives of **liberty** and **justice**. The people did not all sail together. They went to America in **stages**. There was **plenty** of land in America for these people. They also did not have to **depend** on the English government. Instead, they **depended** on themselves. Over time, they worked hard, and a new country **emerged**.

1. Many people in England lived in fear of the government.   _____

2. People could live lives of liberty in America.   _____

3. People did not go to America in stages.   _____

4. People in America depended on England.   _____

135

1 bump
[bʌmp]

v. to run into or hit, often by accident   (syn) crash
bump into
→ I **bumped** into a woman on the street.

2 concrete
[kánkriːt]

n. a hard material used to make buildings   (syn) cement
concrete block
→ They built the house with **concrete** blocks.

3 crack
[kræk]

v. to break without the pieces coming apart
n. a break without the pieces coming apart
crack suddenly → The dish **cracked** suddenly when I dropped it.
small crack → There is a small **crack** in the window.

4 dirt
[dɜːrt]
adj. dirty

n. mud, dust, or soil
remove dirt
→ A washing machine removes **dirt** from clothes.

5 evidence
[évidəns]
adj. evident

n. something that provides proof
show evidence
→ The lawyer showed the **evidence** to the judge.

6 false
[fɔːls]

adj. not correct or true   (syn) wrong
false statement
→ He made a **false** statement to the police.

7 form
[fɔːrm]

n. the shape of a person or thing
v. to make or produce
form of → A starfish has the **form** of a star.
form something → He hopes to **form** a band soon.

8 humorous
[hjúːmərəs]

adj. funny   (syn) comic   (ant) boring
humorous man
→ The comedian is a **humorous** man.

9 indoor
[índɔ̀ːr]

adj. occurring or used in a house or building   (ant) outdoor
indoor sport
→ Squash is an **indoor** sport.

10 joke
[dʒouk]

n. something said or done to make people laugh
tell a joke
→ Anna is good at telling **jokes**.

11 lunar
[lú:nər]

adj. relating to the moon   *(ant)* solar

lunar eclipse

→ There will be a **lunar** eclipse later tonight.

12 male
[meil]

n. a boy or man   *(ant)* female

adj. being a boy or man

be a male → My brother and father are **males**.

male student → The school has many **male** students.

13 medium
[mí:diəm]

adj. of middle size, level, or amount   *(syn)* average

n. a way of communicating information

medium size → Jessica wears a **medium** size.

medium of → TV is a **medium** of communication.

14 positive
[pázətiv]

adj. hopeful, useful, and confident   *(ant)* negative

positive attitude

→ Jeff always has a **positive** attitude.

15 royal
[rɔ́iəl]

adj. relating to a king or queen

royal family

→ The prince is a member of the **royal** family.

16 sticky
[stíki]

adj. having the characteristics of glue

sticky rice

→ They always eat **sticky** rice with their meals.

17 tasty
[téisti]

n. taste

adj. having a good or pleasing flavor   *(syn)* delicious

tasty treat

→ We enjoyed some **tasty** treats during the break.

18 terribly
[térəbli]

adj. terrible

adv. in a very bad manner

terribly sick

→ Rick got **terribly** sick with the flu.

19 western
[wéstərn]

adj. lying in the direction in which the sun sets

western side

→ I live in the **western** side of the city.

20 wood
[wud]

adj. wooden

n. the stem and branches of a tree

chop wood

→ We must chop some **wood** before making a fire.

Unit 28

137

A **Match the words with their definitions.**

1. indoor •   • a. to break without the pieces coming apart

2. terribly •   • b. something that provides proof

3. evidence •   • c. a way of communicating information

4. concrete •   • d. in a very bad manner

5. tasty •   • e. a hard material used to make buildings

6. bump •   • f. occurring or used in a house or building

7. medium •   • g. to run into or hit, often by accident

8. crack •   • h. having a good or pleasing flavor

B **Circle the two words in each group that are opposites.**

1. a. positive   b. false   c. indoor   d. negative

2. a. royal   b. humorous   c. boring   d. medium

3. a. sticky   b. solar   c. lunar   d. tasty

4. a. female   b. dirt   c. crack   d. male

C **Circle the words that best fit the sentences.**

1. He formed | bumped into the vase and knocked it over.

2. They will make a desk from evidence | wood .

3. Everyone laughed at his crack | joke .

4. There is a beach in the western | tasty area of the country.

5. We plan to visit the royal | positive palace on our trip to the city.

6. She always tells false | medium stories to her friends.

D **Choose the correct words to complete the sentences.**

1. Bubble gum can be very _____ after you chew it.
   a. false   b. lunar   c. sticky   d. positive

2. They will _____ a soccer team this summer.
   a. bump   b. form   c. terribly   d. crack

3. That story was _____, so we all laughed.
   a. indoor   b. tasty   c. western   d. humorous

4. There is no _____ he stole the money.
   a. evidence   b. crack   c. wood   d. concrete

5. Please remove the _____ from your hands with soap.
   a. male   b. medium   c. dirt   d. joke

E **Read the passage. Then, fill in the blanks.**

   One day, Mark and Jeff are eating lunch together. They are having **sticky** rice and fried chicken. They think their lunch is very **tasty**. Mark is telling lots of **jokes**. Jeff thinks Mark is very **humorous**. Then, Mark suggests taking a trip during **Lunar** New Year.
Jeff thinks Mark is telling another **joke**, but he is serious.

   The two start making plans for their trip. It is always cold during **Lunar** New Year, and they do not want to visit only **indoor** places. So they decide to visit the **western** part of their country. There, it will be warm, so they can enjoy outdoor activities. Some beautiful **royal** palaces are there. So they can have a chance to visit them. Now they are looking forward to the trip.

1. Jeff and Mark eat _____ rice and fried chicken for lunch.

2. Mark is _____ and likes to tell jokes.

3. Jeff and Mark are going to take a trip during _____ New Year.

4. Jeff and Mark plan to visit the _____ part of their country.

1 bow
[bau]

v. to bend one's head or body to greet someone
bow deeply
→ He **bowed** deeply to his grandparents.

2 direct
[dairékt]
n. direction

v. to manage or guide   (syn) order
adj. moving in a straight line
direct a company → He **directs** a company of 100 people.
direct road → This is a **direct** road to Seoul.

3 disturb
[distɜ́ːrb]

v. to interrupt or bother another person   (syn) annoy
disturb a meeting
→ Do not **disturb** the meeting this time.

4 expect
[ikspékt]

v. to look forward to
expect to
→ I **expect** to see you this evening.

5 grab
[græb]

v. to take hold of something with one's hand
grab something
→ The thief **grabbed** the woman's purse and ran.

6 hardly
[háːrdli]

adv. almost not   (syn) rarely
hardly any
→ There is **hardly** any food in the fridge.

7 knock
[nɑk]

v. to hit a door with one's hand or fist
knock on a door
→ Someone is **knocking** on the door.

8 lock
[lɑk]
n. locker

v. to shut something with a bolt that needs a key to be opened
lock a door
→ Please **lock** the door before you leave.

9 neat
[niːt]
adv. neatly

adj. clean and in good order   (syn) tidy   (ant) messy
neat room
→ My sister always has a **neat** room.

10 nowadays
[náuədèiz]

adv. at the present time   (syn) these days
especially nowadays
→ Pop music has always been popular, especially **nowadays**.

11 obey
[əbéi]

v. to do what someone says   (syn) follow

obey an order

→ Eric **obeyed** the order from the policeman.

12 portrait
[pɔ́:rtrət]

n. a painting, picture, or drawing of a person

paint a portrait

→ The artist is painting a **portrait** now.

13 prefer
[prifə́:r]

v. to like one thing more than another

prefer A to B

→ Lucy **prefers** pizza to sandwiches.

14 senior
[sí:niər]

n. a person older or higher in rank than another   (ant) junior

one's senior

→ Mr. Green is my father's **senior** at work.

15 shelter
[ʃéltər]

n. a place where a person is protected

seek shelter

→ Seek **shelter** if there is a tornado.

16 shout
[ʃaut]

v. to call out loudly   (syn) yell   (ant) whisper

shout at

→ It is not nice to **shout** at people.

17 suggest
[səgdʒést]

n. suggestion

v. to offer a possible plan or idea   (syn) recommend

suggest that

→ Karen **suggested** that everyone eat lunch first.

18 tend
[tend]

v. normally to want to do a certain action

tend to

→ David **tends** to go to bed late on weekends.

19 vet
[vet]

n. an animal doctor

see a vet

→ I took my sick dog to see a **vet**.

20 wrap
[ræp]

v. to cover something with paper or something similar

wrap a present

→ She **wrapped** her present for her brother.

A Circle the words that fit the definitions.

1. to bend one's head or body to greet someone

   a. prefer   b. bow   c. obey   d. direct

2. to take hold of something with one's hand

   a. tend   b. knock   c. grab   d. wrap

3. an animal doctor

   a. senior   b. shelter   c. portrait   d. vet

4. to shut something with a bolt that needs a key to be opened

   a. lock   b. suggest   c. disturb   d. knock

5. to look forward to

   a. shout   b. wrap   c. expect   d. prefer

B Write S for synonym or A for antonym next to each pair of words.

1. _____ shout – whisper   2. _____ hardly – rarely

3. _____ direct – order   4. _____ neat – messy

5. _____ senior – junior   6. _____ suggest – recommend

C Circle the words that best fit the sentences.

1. You should wrap | bow the present to make it look nice.

2. Please prefer | knock on the door before entering.

3. Students should tend | obey the school rules.

4. She disturbed | suggested him while he was studying.

5. They are trying to find an emergency portrait | shelter .

6. Nowadays | Hardly , we use a lot of technology.

D **Choose the correct words to complete the sentences.**

1. I _____ to have sandwiches for lunch.

   a. obey   b. grab   c. knock   d. tend

2. Julie _____ the gold ring to the silver one.

   a. locks   b. prefers   c. bows   d. directs

3. A _____ is hanging on the wall.

   a. portrait   b. senior   c. shelter   d. vet

4. Simon sometimes _____ when he is angry.

   a. wraps   b. suggests   c. shouts   d. disturbs

5. He has _____ any money in his wallet.

   a. nowadays   b. hardly   c. neat   d. direct

E **Read the passage. Then, write T for true or F for false.**

Mary's birthday was coming up, so her friends wanted to buy her a present. Nobody was sure what to buy for her. Todd **suggested** a new bag. Eric thought a **portrait** would be nice. He said that **nowadays**, people **tend** to collect art. Kelly asked Mary's **senior**, and she **suggested** that Mary would want to have a pet.

In the morning on Mary's birthday, somebody **knocked** on the door. She opened the door and saw several of her friends. They all said, "Happy birthday!" Then, they gave Mary her present. It was a puppy. "The **vet** said he is in great health," said Tina. Mary **shouted** with joy and **grabbed** the puppy. "I was not **expecting** this," she said. "Today is the best birthday ever. Thank you so much."

1. Todd suggested buying Mary a new bag. _____

2. Eric wanted to paint a portrait of Mary. _____

3. The vet gave Mary a puppy for her birthday. _____

4. Mary was not expecting to get a puppy. _____

1 bill
[bil]
n. a statement showing money a person owes
pay a bill
→ He pays his car **bill** every month.

2 cast
[kæst]
cast - cast - cast
v. to throw
cast dice
→ The players must **cast** dice during the game.

3 consonant
[kánsənənt]
n. any letter in the alphabet that is not *a, e, i, o,* or *u*   (ant) vowel
consonant sound
→ There are many **consonant** sounds in English.

4 elect
[ilékt]
n. election
v. to choose a person for a position by voting   (syn) select
elect a president
→ The country will **elect** a new president soon.

5 envelope
[énvəlòup]
n. a flat container for a letter
seal an envelope
→ You can seal the **envelope** with glue.

6 fare
[feər]
n. the cost to take a taxi, bus, train, etc.
pay a fare
→ He will pay the **fare** with cash.

7 idiom
[ídiəm]
n. an expression using words with an unexpected meaning   (syn) phrase
common idiom
→ "He is a couch potato" is a common **idiom**.

8 march
[mɑːrtʃ]
v. to walk regular steps like a soldier
march in step
→ All of the soldiers are **marching** in step.

9 motto
[mátou]
n. a saying expressing the beliefs of a person or group
school motto
→ My school **motto** is "Never give up."

NEVER GIVE UP

10 offer
[ɔ́(ː)fər]
v. to say that one is willing to give something   (syn) suggest
offer a job
→ The company decided to **offer** him a job.

11 prevent
[privént]
n. prevention

v. to stop something from happening
prevent an accident
→ Following the rules can **prevent** accidents.

12 prove
[pru:v]

v. to show that something is true   *syn* demonstrate
prove a fact
→ The lawyer **proved** the facts to the judge.

13 rate
[reit]

n. the amount of a payment
v. to guess the value of something
interest rate → The interest **rate** is high these days.
rate a business → Use the survey to **rate** the business.

14 scale
[skeil]

n. a hard plate on animals like fish; the size or extent of something
have scales → All of the fish have **scales**.
large scale → The company makes cars on a large **scale**.

15 score
[skɔ:r]

n. a team's or person's total points in a competition
keep score
→ We must keep **score** to determine the winner.

16 section
[sékʃən]

n. a distinct part of something   *syn* area
section of
→ Soho is a **section** of London.

17 site
[sait]

n. the position or location of a building, city, etc.
building site
→ The building **site** is next to the beach.

18 skip
[skip]

v. to pass over something
skip school
→ He **skipped** school three times last month.

19 staff
[stæf]

n. a group of workers at a business   *syn* employees
big staff
→ There is a big **staff** at the local factory.

20 vowel
[váuəl]

n. any of the letters *a, e, i, o,* or *u*   *ant* consonant
write a vowel
→ The student learned to write the **vowels**.

A **Match the words with their definitions.**

1. envelope •   • a. to show that something is true

2. skip •   • b. to stop something from happening

3. prevent •   • c. the amount of a payment

4. score •   • d. any of the letters *a, e, i, o,* or *u*

5. fare •   • e. a flat container for a letter

6. rate •   • f. a team's or person's total points in a competition

7. prove •   • g. the cost to take a taxi, bus, train, etc.

8. vowel •   • h. to pass over something

B **Circle the two words in each group that have the same meaning.**

1. a. section   b. scale   c. staff   d. area

2. a. cast   b. select   c. prove   d. elect

3. a. offer   b. prevent   c. suggest   d. march

4. a. envelope   b. idiom   c. phrase   d. fare

C **Circle the words that best fit the sentences.**

1. He cast | offered the fishing line into the pond.

2. I can skip | prove that I did not steal the money.

3. The electricity motto | bill was higher last month.

4. "Try your best" is her motto | fare .

5. They are standing on the idiom | site of the old palace.

6. The soldiers can march | prevent 20 kilometers each day.

D Choose the correct words to complete the sentences.

1. _____ are letters such as *d*, *g*, *t*, and *w*.

   a. Consonants   b. Mottos   c. Sites   d. Vowels

2. The _____ on the fish look hard and shiny.

   a. fares   b. scales   c. envelopes   d. sections

3. Everyone on the _____ is working hard today.

   a. idiom   b. bill   c. score   d. staff

4. Janet _____ to help Mark with his report.

   a. offered   b. proved   c. prevented   d. skipped

5. Fred was _____ mayor of the city.

   a. marched   b. rated   c. elected   d. cast

E Read the passage. Then, fill in the blanks.

   Every morning, Greg takes a taxi downtown. He is going to his job **site**. He is a member of the **staff** at a large company. He pays the **fare** and then gets out. He **marches** into the building and goes to his **section**. He handles **bills** the company sends people. He checks each **bill** and makes sure the **rate** is correct. Then, he puts it in an **envelope** and mails it.

Some people think Greg's job is boring, but it is important. He cannot **skip** any **bills**. If a customer cannot pay a **bill**, he **offers** that person a deal. He wants to **prevent** customers from having any problems. Last week, all the employees **cast** their votes to **elect** the employee of the year. The winner was Greg.

1. Greg pays the _____ before he gets out of the taxi.

2. Greg is on the _____ at a large company.

3. Greg cannot _____ any of the customers' bills.

4. Greg was _____ the employee of the year.

A Choose and write the correct words for the definitions.

wrap	bow	rare	justice
proverb	shelter	crack	section

1. the quality of doing what is right ➡ _____

2. to bend one's head or body to greet someone ➡ _____

3. to cover something with paper or something similar ➡ _____

4. to break without the pieces coming apart ➡ _____

5. a distinct part of something ➡ _____

6. not common or hard to find ➡ _____

7. a wise saying ➡ _____

8. a place where a person is protected ➡ _____

B Circle the words that are the most similar to the underlined words.

1. They will ride their bicycles on the <u>trail</u>.
a. liberty   b. tide   c. justice   d. path

2. He often <u>annoys</u> his parents while they are busy.
a. prefers   b. expects   c. wraps   d. disturbs

3. I am looking for the <u>door</u> to the building.
a. grain   b. entrance   c. planet   d. harbor

4. He will <u>demonstrate</u> that he knows the correct answer now.
a. prove   b. cast   c. prevent   d. offer

5. What a <u>delicious</u> meal you made for us!
a. lunar   b. royal   c. tasty   d. humorous

C Choose the correct forms of the words to complete the sentences.

1. The police will collect evident | evidence about the crime.

2. The city residents will elect | election a new mayor next week.

3. Mr. Reynolds' fly | flight to Dallas leaves in one hour.

4. She will lock | locker the door to the office now.

5. He has been poor | poverty for most of his life.

D Complete the sentences with the words in the box.

1. Amy loves _____ such as shrimp and lobster.

2. Glue and honey are both very _____.

3. Try to _____ forest fires when you go camping.

4. Greg _____ to get an A in the class.

5. Everyone _____ on Mr. Arnold for help.

> prevent
>
> depends
>
> seafood
>
> expects
>
> sticky

E Write the correct phrases in the blanks.

plant roots	western side	indoor sports
plenty of	painted a portrait	skip school

1. She _____ of her father.

2. People eat _____ like carrots and radishes.

3. The children enjoy playing _____ in winter.

4. Students should never _____ for any reason.

5. Drink _____ water during hot, sunny weather.

6. The _____ of the country is by the ocean.

F **Circle the mistakes. Then, write the correct sentences.**

1. The students cleaned the classroom and made it neatly.

➡ _____

2. You must blender everything by stirring it together.

➡ _____

3. He did terrible on the test he just took.

➡ _____

4. People usually notice a fast move rather than a slow one.

➡ _____

5. I suggestion that we go inside before it rains.

➡ _____

G **Complete the crossword puzzle.**

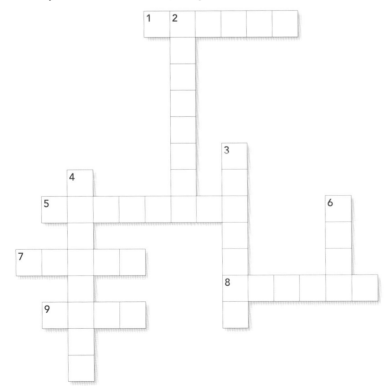

Across

1. happening quickly or unexpectedly
5. a hard material used to make buildings
7. a seed of a plant like rice or corn
8. not including
9. to throw

Down

2. the whole of space and everything in it
3. a place where a person is protected
4. at the present time
6. to pass over something

H   **Read the passage. Then, answer the questions below.**

The Missing Jewels

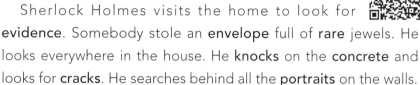

Sherlock Holmes visits the home to look for evidence. Somebody stole an **envelope** full of **rare** jewels. He looks everywhere in the house. He **knocks** on the **concrete** and looks for **cracks**. He searches behind all the **portraits** on the walls.

Then, he walks outside and checks the **ground**. There is a **path**, so he walks along it. It leads to a **cave**. There are **plenty** of places for the thief to **hide** the envelope. But Holmes is **positive** he can find it. There is a **sudden movement** in the **cave**. Holmes rushes over and **shouts** loudly. But he sees nothing in the **cave**.

Holmes returns to the house. He **suggests** that the owner call everyone on the **site**. Holmes looks at the people. He knows who the thief is. Now, he is going to **prove** it.

1. What is the passage mainly about?
    a. the life of Sherlock Holmes
    b. the owner of a home
    c. a secret cave
    d. the search for some missing jewels

2. Where were the jewels?
    a. in an envelope
    b. in a bank
    c. in a safe
    d. in a closet

3. What happens in the cave?
    a. A person runs into it.
    b. There is a sudden movement in it.
    c. Bats fly out of it.
    d. Someone shouts in it.

4. How does Holmes feel about the missing jewels?

    ➡ _____

5. What does Holmes suggest to the owner?

    ➡ _____

151

Index

Index

A

able ⋯⋯⋯⋯⋯ 64
abroad ⋯⋯⋯⋯⋯ 24
absorb ⋯⋯⋯⋯⋯ 80
accident ⋯⋯⋯⋯⋯ 60
achieve ⋯⋯⋯⋯⋯ 36
active ⋯⋯⋯⋯⋯ 16
actual ⋯⋯⋯⋯⋯ 68
adapt ⋯⋯⋯⋯⋯ 84
admire ⋯⋯⋯⋯⋯ 32
adopt ⋯⋯⋯⋯⋯ 96
advertise ⋯⋯⋯⋯⋯ 20
affect ⋯⋯⋯⋯⋯ 84
aim ⋯⋯⋯⋯⋯ 48
alive ⋯⋯⋯⋯⋯ 64
allow ⋯⋯⋯⋯⋯ 92
allowance ⋯⋯⋯⋯⋯ 20
aloud ⋯⋯⋯⋯⋯ 80
amaze ⋯⋯⋯⋯⋯ 12
amount ⋯⋯⋯⋯⋯ 60
ancient ⋯⋯⋯⋯⋯ 84
anger ⋯⋯⋯⋯⋯ 12
animation ⋯⋯⋯⋯⋯ 44
anxious ⋯⋯⋯⋯⋯ 12
apologize ⋯⋯⋯⋯⋯ 32
appear ⋯⋯⋯⋯⋯ 68
apply ⋯⋯⋯⋯⋯ 88
appoint ⋯⋯⋯⋯⋯ 88
appointment ⋯⋯⋯⋯⋯ 16
appreciate ⋯⋯⋯⋯⋯ 104
architect ⋯⋯⋯⋯⋯ 40
area ⋯⋯⋯⋯⋯ 108
argue ⋯⋯⋯⋯⋯ 32
arrest ⋯⋯⋯⋯⋯ 60
arrow ⋯⋯⋯⋯⋯ 48
article ⋯⋯⋯⋯⋯ 88
artificial ⋯⋯⋯⋯⋯ 56
ashamed ⋯⋯⋯⋯⋯ 12
astronaut ⋯⋯⋯⋯⋯ 40
athlete ⋯⋯⋯⋯⋯ 40
atmosphere ⋯⋯⋯⋯⋯ 8
attack ⋯⋯⋯⋯⋯ 48
attempt ⋯⋯⋯⋯⋯ 96
attract ⋯⋯⋯⋯⋯ 116
attractive ⋯⋯⋯⋯⋯ 44
audience ⋯⋯⋯⋯⋯ 44
author ⋯⋯⋯⋯⋯ 40
available ⋯⋯⋯⋯⋯ 24
avenue ⋯⋯⋯⋯⋯ 72
average ⋯⋯⋯⋯⋯ 36
aware ⋯⋯⋯⋯⋯ 80
awkward ⋯⋯⋯⋯⋯ 32

B

background ⋯⋯⋯⋯⋯ 44
backward ⋯⋯⋯⋯⋯ 104
bad ⋯⋯⋯⋯⋯ 60
bare ⋯⋯⋯⋯⋯ 112
base ⋯⋯⋯⋯⋯ 108
beard ⋯⋯⋯⋯⋯ 112
beauty ⋯⋯⋯⋯⋯ 80
beg ⋯⋯⋯⋯⋯ 108
behave ⋯⋯⋯⋯⋯ 32
behind ⋯⋯⋯⋯⋯ 120
benefit ⋯⋯⋯⋯⋯ 20
bet ⋯⋯⋯⋯⋯ 20
bill ⋯⋯⋯⋯⋯ 144
billion ⋯⋯⋯⋯⋯ 20
bite ⋯⋯⋯⋯⋯ 60
bitter ⋯⋯⋯⋯⋯ 80
blame ⋯⋯⋯⋯⋯ 32
blend ⋯⋯⋯⋯⋯ 128
blossom ⋯⋯⋯⋯⋯ 8
border ⋯⋯⋯⋯⋯ 24
bother ⋯⋯⋯⋯⋯ 12
bottom ⋯⋯⋯⋯⋯ 108

bow ⋯⋯⋯⋯⋯ 140
brief ⋯⋯⋯⋯⋯ 68
bubble ⋯⋯⋯⋯⋯ 120
budget ⋯⋯⋯⋯⋯ 20
bullet ⋯⋯⋯⋯⋯ 60
bump ⋯⋯⋯⋯⋯ 136
business ⋯⋯⋯⋯⋯ 20

C

calm ⋯⋯⋯⋯⋯ 80
campaign ⋯⋯⋯⋯⋯ 48
cancel ⋯⋯⋯⋯⋯ 44
cancer ⋯⋯⋯⋯⋯ 16
capital ⋯⋯⋯⋯⋯ 20
capture ⋯⋯⋯⋯⋯ 48
careless ⋯⋯⋯⋯⋯ 60
cart ⋯⋯⋯⋯⋯ 116
cash ⋯⋯⋯⋯⋯ 88
cast ⋯⋯⋯⋯⋯ 144
castle ⋯⋯⋯⋯⋯ 24
caterpillar ⋯⋯⋯⋯⋯ 8
cause ⋯⋯⋯⋯⋯ 16
cave ⋯⋯⋯⋯⋯ 128
celebration ⋯⋯⋯⋯⋯ 44
cell ⋯⋯⋯⋯⋯ 112
century ⋯⋯⋯⋯⋯ 56
certain ⋯⋯⋯⋯⋯ 120
charge ⋯⋯⋯⋯⋯ 20
chase ⋯⋯⋯⋯⋯ 92
cheat ⋯⋯⋯⋯⋯ 36
cheerful ⋯⋯⋯⋯⋯ 12
chemical ⋯⋯⋯⋯⋯ 16
chest ⋯⋯⋯⋯⋯ 112
chief ⋯⋯⋯⋯⋯ 96
choir ⋯⋯⋯⋯⋯ 44
chore ⋯⋯⋯⋯⋯ 96
clap ⋯⋯⋯⋯⋯ 80
clearly ⋯⋯⋯⋯⋯ 56

clever ·········· 36
climate ·········· 8
coast ·········· 24
code ·········· 120
comfort ·········· 24
command ·········· 48
common ·········· 84
community ·········· 32
compare ·········· 92
compete ·········· 36
compose ·········· 40
concentrate ·········· 36
concern ·········· 104
conclusion ·········· 84
concrete ·········· 136
conductor ·········· 40
congratulate ·········· 88
connect ·········· 104
consider ·········· 104
consonant ·········· 144
construction ·········· 72
continent ·········· 108
continue ·········· 116
conversation ·········· 32
cost ·········· 24
cough ·········· 64
countryside ·········· 8
crack ·········· 136
creature ·········· 8
crowd ·········· 108
cultural ·········· 24
curious ·········· 12
custom ·········· 92
customer ·········· 88

D

damage ·········· 48
dare ·········· 120

deaf ·········· 16
death ·········· 16
debate ·········· 84
decorate ·········· 44
dedication ·········· 40
deeply ·········· 68
demand ·········· 104
department ·········· 88
depend ·········· 132
describe ·········· 72
destroy ·········· 48
detail ·········· 84
determine ·········· 96
develop ·········· 96
dew ·········· 128
die ·········· 132
differ ·········· 68
digest ·········· 16
diligent ·········· 40
direct ·········· 140
dirt ·········· 136
dirty ·········· 80
disabled ·········· 60
disadvantage ·········· 88
disagree ·········· 32
disappear ·········· 96
disappoint ·········· 104
discover ·········· 84
discuss ·········· 84
display ·········· 116
distance ·········· 108
disturb ·········· 140
dive ·········· 128
divide ·········· 108
documentary ·········· 84
downstairs ·········· 72
drawer ·········· 72
drug ·········· 16
dull ·········· 12

E

earthquake ·········· 60
ease ·········· 68
education ·········· 85
elbow ·········· 112
elder ·········· 68
elect ·········· 144
electric ·········· 56
electronic ·········· 116
emerge ·········· 132
emergency ·········· 60
emotion ·········· 104
empire ·········· 48
encounter ·········· 24
encourage ·········· 92
enemy ·········· 120
engineer ·········· 40
entrance ·········· 128
envelope ·········· 144
equal ·········· 68
equipment ·········· 40
escape ·········· 120
evidence ·········· 136
exactly ·········· 112
excellent ·········· 36
except ·········· 132
exhibit ·········· 44
exist ·········· 92
exit ·········· 72
expect ·········· 140
expense ·········· 20
experiment ·········· 16
expert ·········· 85
extreme ·········· 56

Index

F

fact 92
false 136
familiar 108
fare 144
fat 64
fear 132
feather 80
fence 108
figure 85
flavor 116
flight 128
flow 80
focus 41
foolish 12
footprint 112
force 132
forecast 56
form 136
fortunate 24
fortunately 120
found 116
frankly 32
freeze 64
front 72
function 17
fur 81
furniture 72

G

gain 21
generally 92
generous 33
genius 36
gentle 12
gift 116

god 132
goods 88
grab 140
grain 128
grateful 13
greenhouse 8
ground 128
growth 17
guard 48
guess 120

H

handkerchief 72
handle 120
happiness 13
harbor 128
hardly 140
harm 17
harvest 8
heat 81
heritage 72
hesitate 104
hide 132
hit 61
hobby 44
horizon 8
host 92
hug 68
huge 112
humorous 136
hunger 17

I

ideal 109
idiom 144
ignore 33

illegal 109
imagine 56
imitate 112
impress 96
include 92
income 21
increase 56
incredible 56
independence 49
indoor 136
infect 112
influence 41
inform 96
information 36
injury 64
insect 8
inspire 33
instruct 93
insult 104
intelligent 41
interview 88
invade 49
invent 41
item 73

J

jaw 113
jewel 116
joke 136
journey 25
joy 121
justice 132

K

kill 49
knock 140

L

laboratory 56
landmark 9
law 89
lecture 85
length 121
liberty 132
lifetime 33
liquid 9
list 93
lively 17
local 25
lock 140
lower 113
lunar 137
lung 113

M

magic 121
mail 116
male 137
manage 41
march 144
marry 33
measure 105
medical 17
medium 137
memorize 96
mess 61
metal 117
method 97
microwave 57
miracle 64
mission 49
modern 57
monster 121

motto 144
movement 133
mystery 45

N

native 25
nearby 25
nearly 93
neat 140
newspaper 41
nickname 68
niece 73
nod 81
normal 69
north 128
notice 93
novel 45
nowadays 140
nutrition 17

O

obey 141
object 117
observe 25
obstacle 49
offer 144
official 109
operation 57
opportunity 21
opposite 69
option 105
order 117
organic 113
organize 41
original 121
outdoor 9

overweight 64
owe 117
owner 97

P

pack 117
pair 69
panic 61
paralyze 61
particular 93
passenger 25
passion 33
path 133
patient 69
perform 121
performance 41
period 21
personal 69
personality 13
persuade 105
physical 17
pimple 64
planet 129
pleasant 9
plenty 133
poison 64
polar 129
pollute 9
poor 133
population 109
portrait 141
position 113
positive 137
pour 81
poverty 21
power 113
practical 89
precious 97

Index

prefer 141
presentation 89
preserve 25
president 109
pretend 45
prevent 145
principal 85
prison 61
private 69
probably 45
produce 97
professional 33
progress 36
promise 105
pronounce 37
proper 65
property 73
prove 145
proverb 133
provide 65
publish 45
purpose 37

Q

quality 81
quarter 21

R

race 113
rapidly 65
rare 129
rate 145
raw 81
realistic 45
realize 69
reasonable 13

recognize 97
recover 17
reflect 97
refuse 117
regret 13
regular 89
relationship 33
relative 105
relax 17
release 121
relieve 65
remain 25
rent 133
repair 73
reply 89
research 37
resource 21
respect 69
responsible 33
return 117
review 37
riddle 85
risk 49
role 41
root 129
royal 137
rub 81

S

safety 93
salary 21
sample 117
satellite 57
scale 145
scare 61
scene 105
scenery 9
scholar 85

scientific 57
score 145
scream 61
script 45
seafood 129
section 145
selfish 105
senior 141
sense 133
separate 89
serve 89
settle 9
shell 129
shelter 141
shock 13
shoot 49
shopkeeper 21
shore 129
shout 141
shy 105
sight 9
sightseeing 25
similar 69
since 93
sincere 105
site 145
situation 45
skip 145
slave 109
smooth 81
sneeze 65
soap 65
soldier 49
solution 37
source 121
southern 129
spaceship 57
spare 73
species 109

spot 97
squeeze 81
staff 145
stage 133
steal 117
sticky 137
stomach 113
subtract 37
successful 41
sudden 133
suggest 141
sunlight 65
supper 73
supply 89
support 21
suppose 85
survey 85
survive 97
swing 73
system 37

T

tasty 137
tax 89
technology 45
teenager 37
telescope 57
tend 141
terribly 137
terrific 69
textbook 37
thumb 113
tide 133
tissue 65
tomb 129
tool 97
total 37
tragedy 61

transport 57
treasure 121
tribe 109
typhoon 9
typical 93

U

unbelievable 61
underground 9
uneasy 13
unhappy 13
unit 109
universe 129
unlike 93
unusual 81
useless 13
usual 73

V

valuable 85
value 97
various 117
vehicle 57
vet 141
victory 49
village 25
violent 49
vision 57
vivid 45
vowel 145

W

war 121
warm 73

wealthy 89
weekly 93
western 137
whisper 105
whole 113
wisdom 13
within 73
wood 137
worried 33
worse 61
worth 109
wound 65
wrap 141

Y

youth 65

Memo